Collage Fusion

VIBRANT WOOD AND FABRIC ART USING TELAMADERA TECHNIQUES

Alma de la Melena Cox

NORTH LIGHT BOOKS
Cincinnati, Ohio

www.mycraftivity.com

D1451505

TELAMADERA FUSION is a trademark which is currently being
examined by the U.S. Patent and Trademark Office and applied
for by Alma de la Melena Cox. All pertinent laws apply herein.

13 12 11 10 09 5 4 3 2 1

Distributed in Canada by Fraser Direct
100 Armstrong Avenue
Georgetown, ON, Canada L7G 5S4
Tel: (905) 877-4411

Distributed in the U.K. and Europe by David & Charles
Brunel House, Newton Abbot, Devon, TQ12 4PU, England
Tel: (+44) 1626 323200, Fax: (+44) 1626 323319
E-mail: postmaster@davidandcharles.co.uk

Distributed in Australia by Capricorn Link
P.O. Box 704, S. Windsor, NSW 2756 Australia
Tel: (02) 4577-3555

De la Melena Cox, Alma.
  Collage fusion : vibrant wood and fabric art using telamadera
techniques / by Alma de la Melena Cox.
       p. cm.
  Includes index.
  ISBN 978-1-60061-330-2 (pbk. : alk. paper)
  1. Collage. 2. Collage--Technique. I. Title.

TT910.D45 2009
702.81'2--dc22
                              2009021036

www.fwmedia.com

EDITOR: Julie Hollyday

DESIGNER: Geoff Raker

PRODUCTION COORDINATOR: Greg Nock

PHOTOGRAPHERS: Christine Polomsky,
Adam Hand

Metric Conversion Chart

to convert	to	multiply by
Inches	Millimeters	25.4
Millimeters	Inches	0.04
Inches	Centimeters	2.54
Centimeters	Inches	0.4
Feet	Centimeters	30.5
Centimeters	Feet	0.03
Yards	Meters	0.9
Meters	Yards	1.1
Sq. Inches	Sq. Centimeters	6.45
Sq. Centimeters	Sq. Inches	0.16
Sq. Feet	Sq. Meters	0.09
Sq. Meters	Sq. Feet	10.8
Sq. Yards	Sq. Meters	0.8
Sq. Meters	Sq. Yards	1.2
Pounds	Kilograms	0.45
Kilograms	Pounds	2.2
Ounces	Grams	28.3
Grams	Ounces	0.035

Dedication

I dedicate this book to my family. Mike, you show me daily what love looks like. Thank you for always believing in what is possible. I am so grateful we share this life together. Rachel, you encourage me to dream my love. Riley, you show me that imagination and humor know no bounds. Mom and Dad, I see my life as an adventure because of you. Julie and Mike Vondergeest, and Lee, Marilyn, Doug, Eden, Kevin and Ryan Cox, I'm grateful for your presence in my life. I love you all.

Acknowledgments

The efforts of many talented and generous individuals at North Light Books made this book possible and I am very grateful to all of them. In addition, I'd like to thank Christine Doyle for seeing the possibility in my artwork; Tonia Davenport for her guidance; Christine Polomsky for sharing her gift of beautiful photography; Geoff Raker for his design talent; and, especially, Julie Hollyday for her editorial, communication and organizational skills, and for her creativity.

Photo by Rachel Cox

About the Author

Alma de la Melena Cox is an award-winning quilter whose passion for fabric led her to create Telamadera Fusion, a collage process of bringing fabric and wood together. Her images have been used for clothing, book cover artwork and greeting cards. She recently created a line of rubber stamps. She has been featured on the television show *Oregon Art Beat*, and in several publications including *Bend Living*, *Cloth Paper Scissors* and *Quilting Arts* magazines. Alma's artwork is in numerous collections in the U.S. and abroad. She enjoys gallery representation and often participates in juried art shows. She is a self-taught, mixed-media artist who enjoys teaching her techniques and loves making artwork.

Alma's studio and home is in Sisters, Oregon, where she lives with her husband, Mike, their two children and their dog, Augustus. When not creating art, she enjoys traveling with her family and spending time with her friends. To see more of her work, please visit www.almaart.com.

Contents

Detail of *Angel*

Introduction

You've picked up this book because you are traveling on a creative path. Maybe you want to try something new, you want to bring more creativity into your life or you are an artist seeking to expand your techniques. Whatever place you're coming from, I welcome you!

When I was younger, there were kids in school who could draw amazing cartoons and realistic drawings of anything they wanted. They were called "gifted." As a child, I had a sense that my gifts would be revealed to me one day, the way some kids discovered they could run really fast or were whizzes at math. It was 25 years before I would realize the gift: That art can be made by anyone and everyone, with or without the ability to render something realistic.

The projects and techniques you'll see in this book evolved from my passion for bringing the unlikely elements of fabric and wood together in a process I call Telamadera Fusion. With Telamadera Fusion, you can create brilliantly colored and luminous artwork no matter your level of expertise. The words *collage, mixed-media* and *fusion* excite me with their limitless potential as materials are combined to make my heart sing. I'll show you how to take imagery, the brilliant colors of fabrics, paints and papers, mixed with contrast, layers and sparkle to create inspired artwork.

As the ideas for this book developed, I saw that each idea led to the next one; it was like opening a gift and finding another one inside. I am grateful for the opportunity to hand the box to you so that you may unwrap it and add to all the possibilities. I hope you have fun as we navigate the path together.

Detail of *Reclaiming Yin 2*

Materials

Telamadera Fusion brings fabric and wood together by fusing them. Although many projects were inspired by this technique, not all of them require fabric or wood. You'll find projects on canvas, fabric and cardstock, and you can create with paper and paint if you prefer.

Wood

My love of trees has required me to ask myself if creating art with wood is in the best interest of our planet. I think it is important to know our wood sources and to make sure it is not coming from precious, endangered rain forests. We should use sustainable and engineered wood products as much as we can and buy from suppliers that are committed to preserving this valuable resource.

Pine or Basswood (pre-routed)

You have the option to obtain pre-routed pieces inexpensively from craft supply stores to get started on a project right away. I recommend using an 11" × 11" (28cm × 28cm) piece of wood for your first-time project; it's what I use when teaching workshops. These are useful if you do not have the tools necessary to cut and rout your own wood. In general they are categorized as wood plaques. They are sold in various sizes and shapes. I recommend this route for your first Telamadera Fusion artwork. In my experience many hardware and wood suppliers are helpful in cutting larger wood pieces, sometimes for a small fee.

Other Woods

You can find laminated pine in large pieces that can be cut and routed to suit your size needs. You can use ½" (1cm) thickness for smaller pieces, but I recommend 1" (3cm) thickness for artwork larger than 18"×18" (46cm × 46cm). Routing is optional. Other wood, such as birch plywood, works well in ¼" (6mm) thickness for smaller pieces and ½" (1cm) thickness for larger than 24 × 24 (61cm × 61cm). I like to create a simple wood frame around this kind of wood because of its rough edges as in *Between and Within* (page 48). See the instructions for *Listen* (page 84) for framing thinner pieces of wood. For that project I used a craft frame made of melamine. You can also use craft wood shapes to embellish larger pieces of art and to make

jewelry. Virtually any lumber wood can be used for Telamadera Fusion. I have personally liked working with ½" (1cm) and 1" (3cm) laminated pine and ¼" (6mm) birch plywood the best. I routed several of the pieces in this book with either a ⅜" (9mm) rabbeting router bit for a contemporary look or a ¼" (6mm) cove router bit for a traditional look. Many were left without routing, too.

Fabrics

It can be a little daunting to walk into a fabric store for the first time and face thousands of options. I have found that 100 percent cotton fabrics work best. Most metallic fabrics work, too, although they are delicate (we will get to that later). I love using metallic fabrics and I encourage you to venture to the section of the store that I call "the Junior Prom Shiny's" to find the fabrics that are used for fancier dresses for weddings, proms, etc.

The smallest amount of fabric you can buy (have cut) is ⅛ yard (11cm). You may also buy fabric in increments of ¼, ½, ⅝ and ¾ of a yard (23, 46, 57 and 69cm) or entire yards. Many fabric stores sell fabric already cut into "fat quarters." This is fabric that is a quarter of a yard cut into a larger square shape instead of a long, skinny strip. You can ask a salesperson to cut a fat quarter for you, however you'll pay slightly more if you take this route. The advantage to this cut is that you have a piece of fabric that is wider, which can be beneficial if you have a larger pattern that you want to use.

Steam-A-Seam 2

This is fusible webbing found online and in fabric stores. I have found that this particular double-sided fusible webbing fuses to wood very well. You'll find it sold in small packages with sheets sized 8½" × 11" (22cm × 28cm). In some fabric stores you can find it in a large roll; bring the entire roll to a salesperson to have it cut for you. There are many fusible webbing products on the market today and many may work for this process, however, I have not tried anything besides Steam-A-Seam 2 (SAS2).

Paints

Acrylic-based paints work best for this type of art-work. Acrylic paint comes in a huge selection of colors, and with paint mixing, the color possibilities are truly endless.

Liquitex High Gloss Varnish

The last step of the Telamadera Fusion process requires a lot of varnishing. I like the Liquitex High Gloss Varnish because it is made for fine art, is archival, does not yellow and has UV protection. It is self-leveling and polymer-based. Pour the varnish into a clean plastic container when varnishing a piece—the unused varnish can be poured back into the original bottle as long as it is clean.

Use an exterior water-based varnish for art-work you want to hang outside. Simply apply two final coats over the ten coats of Liquitex High Gloss Varnish.

Other Materials

Telamadera Fusion art can be as fun and artistic as you want it to be. This book features *Additional Techniques* (see pages 26–64) that expand the Telamadera Fusion process to give your art extra depth, texture and beauty. Here are a few highlights of items you can use:

Additional Wood Elements

There are many pre-made wood craft items to choose from that lend themselves well to the Telamadera Fusion process. Wood photo albums make a great canvas; small craft wood shapes are wonderful for adding dimension and making jewelry; and even craft frames made of melamine can be a wonderful starting point for a piece. Wood cubes, wood dowels and mini clothespins are easy to find online and in craft stores. Wood trims can be found at large home supply and lumber stores.

Embellishments

If you think your artwork needs a little some-thing extra, these embellishments really make a piece pop. I love using dimensional paint to add another layer of texture to my artwork. Glitter, beads, tiny mirrors and crystals all add sparkle and shine. There is even a chance to use objects like glass, shells, keys and anything else you can think of!

Scrapbooking Elements

Steam-A-Seam 2 works great with many kinds of specialty papers and scrapbook papers. Cardstock is a heavier paper that you can apply paint to without worry of warping. Lace cardstock can add a lovely texture to your art's background.

Rub-on transfers, a favorite with scrap-bookers, can be layered on top of painted surfaces. Rubber stamps and foam stamps are also an inexpensive and easy way to add interest to your backgrounds. When using rubber stamps, use permanent inks because they don't smear when you varnish over them. All these items can be found online or in your local craft stores.

Other Artists' Materials

The Telamadera Fusion process meshes so well with other art forms, from wearable jewelry to silkscreening original designs, and there's a way to incorporate it into any medium. The projects in this book (pages 72–119) feature a range of artistic supplies. Encaustic, a simple screen print, collage work, sewing and more are all represented.

Adhesives

Adhesives are used to add embellishments and wood pieces. I recommend having several types on hand: A strong adhesive, such as Aleene's 7800, a glue stick and wood glue.

Tools

Just as with the materials used in Telamadera Fusion art, the tools can range from the most basic to those that necessitate muscling your own corner of the garage tool space. The optional items listed here reflect a portion of the tools needed for the additional techniques and some of the projects. Read each technique and project materials list carefully for the full list of what you'll need.

Basic Telamadera Fusion Tools

To successfully complete the basic Telamadera Fusion project (page 14), you will need the following supplies:

Wood Burning Tool

You can find a basic wood burning tool online or at your local craft store. You can often find one that comes with several tips. I use the universal tip for most wood burning, but I also find opportunities to use the fine tip. I encourage you to use scrap pieces of wood to practice wood burning before taking it to a project. Make sure your wood burning tool reaches at least 900°F (482°C).

Technically speaking, a wood burning tool is optional when creating Telamadera Fusion art; paint and images can work just as well in defining spaces for fabric, like in *Copyright Free Image* (page 36). But I do love to use the wood burning tool to add the depth and texture I mentioned above.

Iron

A household iron works well, but make sure its water chamber is empty because steam should not be used. I recommend a separate iron just for Telamadera Fusion work because a small artistic mishap could help to ruin your clothes!

Breathing Mask

Please wear one when fusing fabric to wood. Many craft paints are nontoxic, but it's best to be overly cautious when applying heat to a painted surface with the iron.

Paintbrushes

You'll need two types of brushes.

Regular artist's paintbrushes are used to paint the Telamadera Fusion artwork. These come in many sizes and styles, so choose the ones you like to work with that also work well with acrylics paints.

A medium-sized, high-quality paintbrush is used for varnishing. I have found that a higher quality interior house paintbrush works well for varnishing as it minimizes bubbles and, when rinsed thoroughly after each use, will last a long time. After each use, soak the paintbrush overnight in clean water, rinse it off and let it air dry completely. I like to have two brushes—I can use one while the other dries.

Fine-Tipped, Sharp Fabric Scissors

Dedicate a pair of scissors to fabric to keep them sharp. I prefer small scissors because they are easy to handle when cutting detailed and small shapes.

Paper and Pencil

Simple paper and pencil are the basis for almost all Telamadera Fusion artwork. Use these basic but crucial tools to map out your designs. Your drawings can be enlarged or reduced to fit your design ideas by using the enlarge function on a copy machine or by scanning the image into your computer and using your favorite image-editing software.

Carbon Paper

Carbon paper can help take your design from a sketch to a full Telamadera art piece. It is found at most office supply stores.

Permanent Markers

I recommend fine-tipped markers in black and another bold color like red or blue. Use these markers to trace over your designs and help transfer the design to the Steam-A-Seam 2. Permanent marker does not smear on the backing paper of the Steam-A-Seam 2 when it is ironed to fabric as pencil does, leaving the lines clearly visible for cutting.

Fine Grit Sandpaper

The Telamadera Fusion technique works best with smooth pieces of wood. You should sand all of the wood surfaces, including the back and the edges. Wear the breathing mask if the wood piece must be sanded a lot.

Scrap Cloth

A small piece of cotton cloth placed between the iron and the fabric to be fused to the wood keeps your iron clean and the fabric protected. A piece of an old sheet works well for this.

Paper Towels

Keep a roll handy to clean up messes. You can use a few layers of paper towels as scrap cloth in a pinch.

Optional Tools

These items are necessary only when you want to add media and special touches to your Telamadera Fusion artwork. You should read each additional technique and project for specific tools, but here is a list of some the basic items:

Power Tools

Using ready-made wood products and pieces is a great way to get started with Telamadera Fusion, but you may want a little more control over the wood you use when you become more involved in creating your own Telamadera Fusion art pieces.

An electric wood saw and electric wood router will give you more control over your designs. Power drills come in handy when adding various embellishments to your art pieces. Follow all the manufacturer's directions when operating these power tools. If you have never used power tools I highly recommend you seek an experienced person to teach you how to use them. Large home supply stores sometimes offer classes, too. Always wear protective eyewear when you are operating power tools.

Hand Saw and Miter Box

A hand saw and miter box make cutting wood pieces so much easier. These low-tech tools make clean cuts and beautiful angles. Just as with the electric tools, you should follow the manufacturer's instructions and use the saw with caution.

Teflon Pressing Sheet

A Teflon pressing sheet is wonderful to have when you're layering various media in Telamadera Fusion art—it keeps those products from adhering to the iron when you're fusing fabric. I recommend having a sheet on hand so you can layer without hesitation. Follow the instructions closely to protect the iron, the Teflon sheet and the artwork.

Small Wood Clamps

If you decide to add wood trims or pieces to you artwork, wood clamps will guarantee a strong bond.

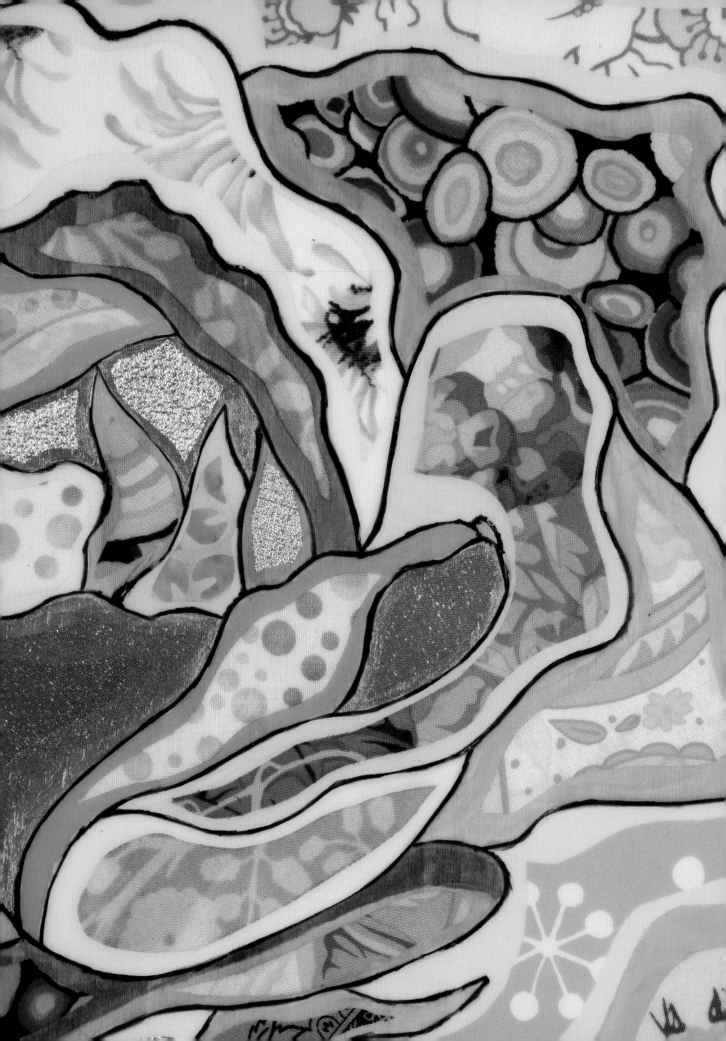

Techniques

Telamadera Fusion had its beginnings in a sandwich board that changed my life.

When setting up for an art festival, I used fabric to spell the words *Alma Art* and adhered them to the wood of a sandwich board sign. At the festival, I displayed my art quilts for the first time and learned my first real art lesson: Not everyone will like your stuff.

A group of women came into my booth and proceeded to discuss their dislike for my work—in Spanish. Perhaps they thought I couldn't understand them, but since I know the language, every word pinched my artist soul. Among all the negative remarks, one of the women said, "This is the only thing I like here," as she glanced past my quilts and pointed to my sign. I was heartbroken. Some might think me naive, and I would agree, but I am also a sensitive soul who took it personally. It was the first time I had heard negative comments about my work.

It took a few days for me to remember that making art makes me deeply happy. I can't say that I always see the glass half full but I'm grateful for those people in my life who sometimes force me to do so. That's when the sandwich board spoke and said, "I *am* pretty cool." Well, not literally, but it did have my attention. So began my journey of bringing fabric and wood together.

After a few months of trial and error, I figured out how to combine wood and fabric into beautiful archival-quality artwork. To honor my heritage, I gave the process a name inspired by words in Spanish: *Tela*, meaning fabric, and *madera*, meaning wood. Fusing these elements inspired the techniques that follow. They evolved as my curiosity led me to try things beyond the surface.

It has been a fun ride that I hope you'll join me for. I have had the opportunity to teach this technique to seasoned artists, to elementary school children and to people in different places along their creative path. I love watching individuals bring their unique view to this process and seeing the creative door open for them the way the sandwich board opened mine.

Detail of *The Rose*

Telamadera Fusion

Telamadera Fusion is the main recipe for the techniques that follow and will demonstrate how to fuse fabric to wood to make it sing in a whole new way. You will see new depth in the fabric and wood as you collage different elements together, all topped with polymer-based varnish.

I intentionally used many fabrics in *The Rose* to illustrate how easy the Telamadera Fusion process is to follow, whether there are many fabrics or a few. Please read these instructions as the other techniques will often reference this one.

THE ROSE
With its many fabrics, colors and textures, I hope The Rose *will inspire you to let your creativity blossom!*

Materials

15" × 15" (38cm × 38cm) wood plaque or laminated pine

clamps (optional)

router with ¼" (6mm) bit (optional)

protective eyewear for routing

fine grit sandpaper

paper

pencil

black fine-tipped permanent marker

red fine-tipped permanent marker (or another color other than black)

carbon paper

breathing mask

wood burning tool with universal tip

small and medium paintbrushes (flat works best)

acrylic paints

Steam-A-Seam 2 (SAS2)

scissors

assorted cotton and metallic fabrics

iron

ironing surface

scrap cloth

cellophane tape

ruler

Phillips head screwdriver

2 D-rings with mounting plates for screws

screws that fit the D-rings

picture hanging wire, approx. 6.2mm

wire cutters

Liquitex High Gloss Varnish

medium Purdy brush

plastic container

14

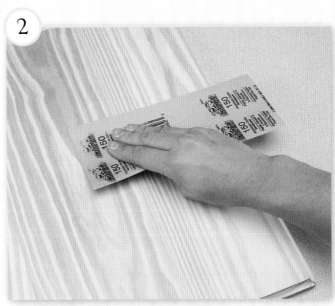

Rout wood (optional)
Using the clamps, secure the wood to the work surface. With the router on and locked, keep the router plate flush with the surface and move it away from you along the edge of the wood. Repeat with all edges, turning the router off and reclamping the wood if necessary.

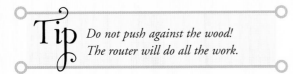

Tip *Do not push against the wood! The router will do all the work.*

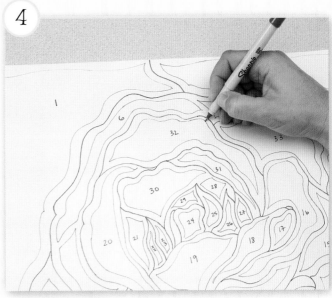

Sand wood
Using the sandpaper, gently smooth the wood's surface. Going with the grain, sand the front of the piece, the back of the piece and then the sides.

Prepare design
Using the pencil, draw the design on the paper. Leave lots of open spaces to show the layering of the paint and the fabric. This will allow for a paint border around the fabric later in the process.

Continue design
Using the black marker, number the drawing sections as you see fit. The black lines represent the spaces that will be painted. Using the red marker, draw outlines within the open spaces where the fabric will go. Leave a ⅛"–¼" (3mm–6mm) space between the red and black lines.

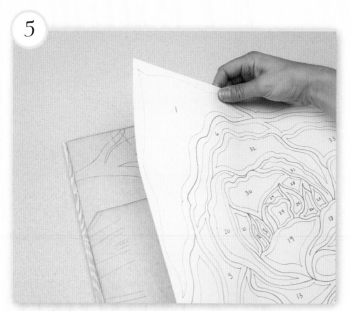

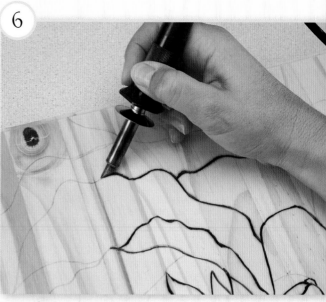

Trace design onto wood

Place the carbon paper onto the wood piece and layer the drawing on top. Using the pencil, trace the black lines of the design onto the wood.

Burn design into wood

Safety first: Wear the breathing mask and follow all the manufacturer's directions and safety regulations. The tip of the wood burning tool will heat up to 900°F (482°C), so take every precaution.

Using the wood burning tool with a universal tip, burn the lines of the design you would like to emphasize. Use gentle pressure and a gliding motion to burn the wood.

When you are finished using the tool, turn it off, unplug it and allow it to cool away from children and pets.

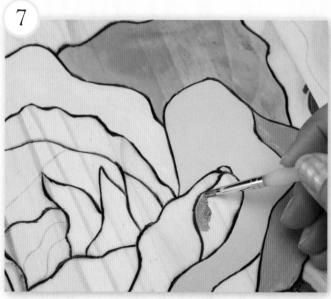

Paint wood

Using the paintbrush, paint the wood with the acrylic paints within the lines you burned in Step 6. If desired, paint the sides and back of the wood piece (I painted the back of the wood panel black). Let the paint dry thoroughly before adding the fabric in Step 12.

Tip

Practice using the wood buring tool on a scrap piece of wood to get the feel of it. Wood burning cannot be rushed, so patience and practice go a long way. For the best results, avoid pushing the metal tip into the wood and keep a mild and even pressure when burning the lines.

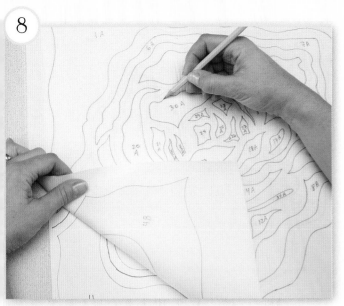

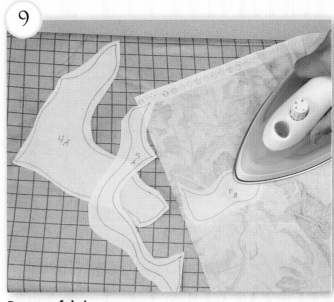

Prepare Steam-A-Seam 2

Lay the piece of Steam-A-Seam 2 (SAS2) on top of the paper with the design. Using the black marker, trace along the red lines onto the SAS2. Label these pieces with the corresponding number and an A (for example 1A, 2A, 3A and so on).

Turn the piece of SAS2 over. Using the marker, retrace the design that is showing through from the opposite side. Label this side with the corresponding number and a B (for example, 1B, 2B, 3B and so on).

Prepare fabric

Using the scissors, cut out all SAS2 pieces leaving at least a 1/8" (3mm) border around the drawn line. Taking one piece at a time, remove the paper from the side marked A. (The paper on the B side stays on at this time.) Place the fusible webbing directly on the wrong side of the fabric. (The B side paper is now face up.) Using the iron on a cotton setting, iron the B side paper with an even pressure until the SAS2 is fused to the fabric.

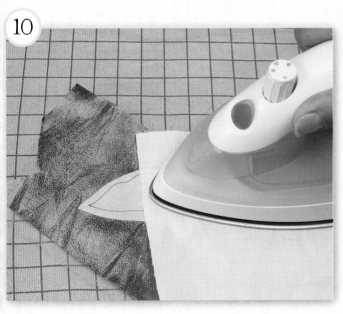

 If you're having trouble seeing the lines through the Steam-A-Seam 2 when tracing the image onto it, place the drawing against a window to use the sun as a backlight.

Ironing metallic fabrics

Follow the same instructions in Step 9 up until ironing the fabrics. For metallic fabrics, use a wool heat setting and place a scrap cloth between the iron and the SAS2. (Without the scrap cloth, the metallic fabric could melt and ruin your iron.)

11

Trim pieces

Using the scissors, trim the fused fabric pieces on the black line.

12

Apply fabric to wood

Carefully remove the SAS2 side B backing paper from the fabric. Place the fabric piece (fusible side down) in its corresponding painted space until you have placed all the fabric pieces on the surface.

Tip *If you're having trouble removing the Steam-A-Seam 2 backing from the already-fused fabric, try using a straight pin to score the backing.*

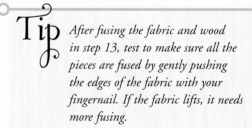

Tip *After fusing the fabric and wood in step 13, test to make sure all the pieces are fused by gently pushing the edges of the fabric with your fingernail. If the fabric lifts, it needs more fusing.*

Tip *Steam-A-Seam 2 will adhere more than just fabric to the wood. Try papers, smooth (not bumpy) laces, trims and ribbons for a touch of your personal style.*

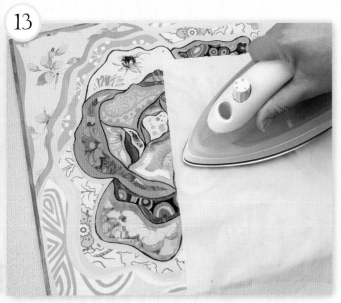

Fuse fabric to wood

Place the scrap cloth between the artwork and the iron. Using the iron on a wool setting, fuse the fabric to the wood by placing the iron on an area for a few seconds, then lifting it up and moving it to another area. Repeat this step until all the fabric is fused to the wood.

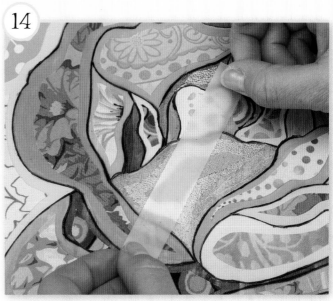

Remove debris

Gently press a piece of cellophane tape onto the surface of the wood-fabric piece and to remove any debris on the surface. If pieces of the fabric lift with the tape, repeat Step 13 to fuse the fabric completely.

Apply varnish

Pour a small amount of varnish into the plastic cup. Using the Purdy brush, apply the varnish over the entire piece. Allow the varnish to dry for 24 hours. Repeat this step until ten coats of varnish have been applied. Apply only one coat of varnish to the back.

Tip

When you add the first few coats of varnish, you'll wonder why it looks so crummy. But have no fear, just keep going! The fabric will soak up the varnish until it reaches its saturation point. After that, the varnish will sit on top of the fabric, and that's where the glossy look comes from. I like ten coats of varnish on my artwork, but you'll start to see a difference after about six coats.

Avoid brushing too much— one or two passes over an area is enough. Brushing too much might make the varnish dry with a cloudy look.

Liquitex High Gloss Varnish is self-leveling so work on a flat surface. Otherwise the varnish will pool in the corners of trapped spaces.

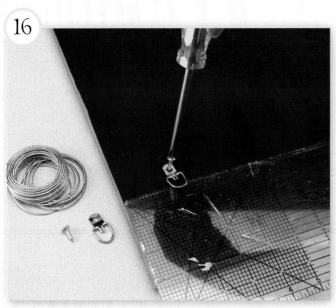

Apply hardware to the back

When all the layers of varnish have dried, turn the artwork over. Using the ruler, measure 3" (8cm) down from the top and 2" (5cm) in from the side. Using the pencil, mark this spot. Repeat for the other side.

Using the Phillips head screwdriver and screws, secure the D-rings with mounting plates in the marked spots.

Secure hanging wire

Using the wire cutters, cut approximately 2½' (76cm) of the picture wire. Thread the wire through the D-Ring and twist to secure it. Secure the same piece of wire to the D-ring on the other side.

Tip

In general place the D-ring with mounting plate a quarter of the way down from the top of the art piece and a few inches (centimeters) in, perhaps 2"–3" (5cm–8cm), from the sides. Make sure the wire, when secure, is well below the top of the piece so it remains unseen.

Gallery

IN MY VIEW
Telamadera Fusion

SACRED GARDEN

Telamadera Fusion

FLOWERS ON GOLD
Telamadera Fusion

RANUNCULUS
Telamadera Fusion

LITTLE HOUSE OF LOVE
Telamadera Fusion

Additional Techniques

In the same way that the sandwich board opened the door for me to fuse fabric to wood, Telamadera Fusion opens even more possibilities that you'll find in the following techniques.

Wood is a great substrate to experiment with. Not only can it be purchased in craft form—like the photo album used in *Stencils for Fabric* (page 38)—it also can be cut to any shape and size to suit your work. It can be drilled into, as in *Embedding Mirrors* (page 46), and its beauty can be emphasized, as in *Transparent Paint* (page 32).

I can't help but think that wood and fabric were just waiting to be put together to express a new kind of beauty. My ever-growing collection of fabrics yields yummy palettes and gorgeous colors. Begin growing your own fabric stash and get inspired to use it up by making your own *Custom Paint Swatches* (page 33) or by using *Stencils for Fabric* (page 38) to lend a great design to a great fabric. Paper and other embellishments can add touches of whimsy sure to delight: *Dimensional Paint* (page 50) can add emphasis and color, while a *Collage Background* (page 40) can add overall interest to your art.

I know you'll fall in love with discovering all the fabulous combinations for your own beautiful art.

Detail of *Be The Light*

Add Texture With Wood Burning

The wood burning tool outlines, but it can also create interesting textures that emphasize elements of your artwork and draw the viewer in. Transparent acrylics and water work best to paint right over the burned marks.

Materials

wood burning tool with universal tip

RECLAIMING YIN 2

I had a tire swing when I was nine that hung from an old oak tree. Some of my most blissful moments were spent there at an age when I thought anything was possible—like a tree seed I was bursting with potential. As I grew, my roots grounded me, and as I age, my creativity blossoms.

Can you recall what was possible in your childhood daydreams? How can you celebrate those possibilities in your artwork today?

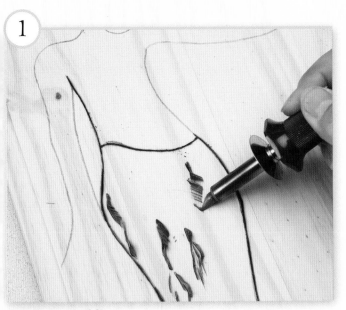

1

Create jagged lines

Follow the instructions for transferring a design in the Telamadera Fusion process (pages 16–17).

Using the wood burning tool, outline the contour lines of the drawn object.

By leaning the wood burning tool from side-to-side, you can create jagged lines.

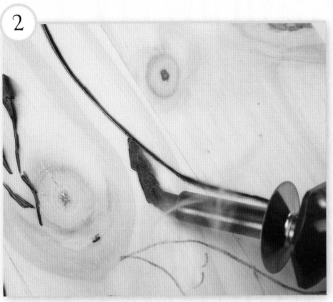

2

Create deep grooves

Leave the wood burning tool on the wood for a longer amount of time to create deeper grooves.

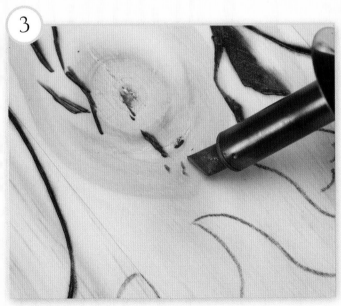

3

Create color variations

Slowly drag the tip of the tool on its side down the surface of the wood to darken large areas. Lightly drag the tool for less time to create color variations.

Continue with the Telamadera Fusion process. Varnishing will highlight and bring out the various colors in the textured area.

Tip

I use this technique a lot to add a special element to my designs that incorporate trees. I like to pair this with the Transparent Paint technique (page 32) to achieve wonderful coloring while still using the natural wood grain.

Wood Burning Words

The wood burning tool, with its many different tips, is quite versatile. You can make the smallest marks with a fine tip. It's perfect for small words, characters, facial features and for shading in small areas.

PEACE

"All true artists, whether they know it or not, create from a place of no-mind, from inner stillness."

—Eckhart Tolle

I find that wood burning can be a meditative process. I like to sit on our deck in the summer with a few projects to burn and see what the Muse brings me.

Materials
Wood burning tool with fine tip point

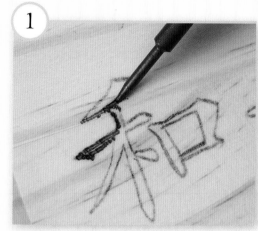

1 Create texture with fine tip
Transfer the design following the Telamadera Fusion process.
When burning small designs with many curves and turns, the fine tip works best.

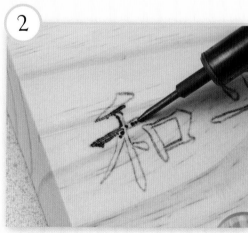

2 Add shading
You can add shading or color by lightly burning small points with the tip of the tool.
Finish the piece following the Telamadera Fusion process.

Wood Grain Design

No two fingerprints are alike and neither is the grain we see in cut planks of wood. Engineered wood, such as plywood and laminated varieties, create even more variation as several wood grains are merged to create a larger piece and, therefore, more design opportunities! This free-style technique is used at the very beginning of the Telamadera Fusion process and acts as a basis for the design.

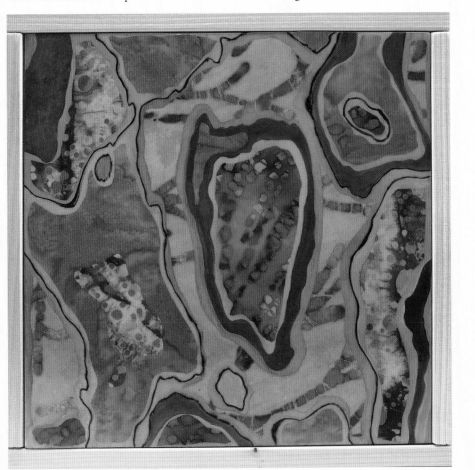

Materials

½" (1cm) thick plywood, cut to desired size

sandpaper

pencil

BETWEEN AND WITHIN

Spend time selecting wood pieces you find interesting. There might be a landscape waiting to be outlined or abstract shapes waiting to be discovered. It's fun to go through scrap piles of wood at building sites, but ask first! I have found that many builders are happy to cut pieces for me (let them know you're an artist) and sometimes they point me toward a particularly interesting piece.

Choose wood piece

Choose the piece of wood that speaks to you. Look at both sides of the panel, turn it around and upside down. I chose this piece of wood because it had large organic shapes that I found inspiring.

Identify design

Using the sandpaper, sand the plywood thoroughly as it tends to have a rougher surface than other woods. Select some of the lines of the grain that appeal to you. Using the pencil, trace over those grain lines, creating spaces large enough to paint and place fabric on.

Continue with the Telamadera Fusion process.

Tip

If you're having trouble seeing the wood grain, it sometimes helps to brush a little water onto the surface. Let the water dry before continuing with the Telamadera Fusion process.

Transparent Paint

This technique is a favorite of mine and it's easy to do. Water mixed with transparent acrylic paint enhances the wood grain, creating depth. Sanding the wood surface until it is smooth as a first step helps to create this beautiful design element.

Materials

2 small bowls

transparent acrylic paint

water

paintbrush

scrap paper

CLIFF HOUSE

When I was five I lived in a house on stilts, on a cliff, overlooking the ocean. I felt like a flying bird when I rode my red tricycle on our long deck. My school, called Alma Heights (truly!), had the longest, fastest slide, brilliantly built into the side of the hill. Sitting at the top overlooking the ocean, it seemed like I'd slide right into the water.

What events in your childhood brought you wonder and awe? Whether it was your first splash in the pool or listening to your grandfather tell stories, incorporate it into your artwork and see what beautiful images a memory can produce.

Prepare paint and surface

This technique should be completed after burning the lines on the art piece but before adding any paints or fabrics (see pages 15–16, step 1–6).

In one bowl, mix a very small amount of the transparent paint with water. Fill the other bowl with clean water. Using a clean paintbrush, apply a generous amount of clean water to the portion of the surface you will be painting.

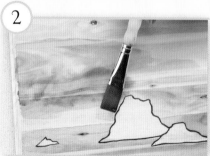

Apply paint

Using the paintbrush, paint the desired area with a small amount of the diluted paint, working quickly so the paint is applied evenly throughout the area. Brush the paint within ½" (1cm) of the burned lines and let the paint "travel" to them. The wood burned lines act as gutters to keep the water from spreading, but too much water could travel beyond the burned lines. (Do not let the water pool.)

Let the background dry completely before continuing with the Telamadera Fusion process.

Tip

Test the paint on a piece of scrap paper; add more paint to darken the color or more water to lighten it.

It is easy to stain the wood, so a little paint goes a long way. Let the wood do the work for you, as it will naturally spread the paint.

Custom Paint Swatches

Fabric stores have cleverly taken the guesswork out of buying fabrics that harmonize by creating what they call fat quarter bundles, coordinated fabric six-packs for your ease and enjoyment. Take your bundle with you as you make your paint selection and contrast the fabrics with different background paint colors. When using this technique with the Telamadera Fusion process, it's not necessary to wood burn to create a beautiful piece.

Materials

fat quarter bundle

acrylic paints

paintbrush

paper

NEW YORK BEAUTY

Traditional quilt blocks like this one are great for their inherent graphic design. Many are copyright-free, easy to trace and, in Telamadera Fusion, don't require multiple blocks to create high impact on your wall. If you're a beginner, create custom swatches until you find a combination that sings to you. If you're a seasoned artist, challenge yourself with fabrics and colors you've never worked with before.

Tip

Look to lesser-used colors in the fabric pattern when deciding which paints to use for the background. You can add white or black paint to the colors you choose to create more contrast. For example, a fabric with some fuchsia in it might lead you to match a fuchsia paint color, but a better way would be to add white to make it pink, keeping it in the color family without overwhelming your piece.

Depending on the design, you can use as few as three paint colors or as many as you'd like to pair with the fabrics in the artwork.

1

Paint swatches

Identify four to five colors that correspond to the fabric. Using the paintbrush and acrylic paints, paint a block of each color onto the paper. Use this paper as your reference while you design your piece by swapping fabric pieces among the paint swatches.

Copyright-Free Image

There are several online sources for copyright-free images. I obtained this one from www.karenswhimsy.com. Before using any copyright free image, be sure to read the Terms of Use. Some images cost money and some do not. See the Resources (page 126) for other copyright-free image sources.

Materials

copy of desired image

fine-tipped scissors

black fine-tipped permanent marker

Steam-A-Seam 2 (SAS2)

DOLLY

Create artwork without drawing at all! Add shapes to your scrapbook pages, too, with beautiful fabrics. You can iron them right onto your paper. Combine this technique with the Exaggerating Size technique (page 36) to personalize your photos in a special wall hanging.

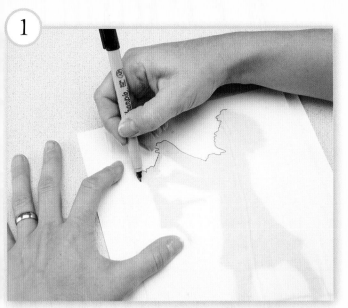

Prepare image

Choose a copyright-free image. Using a computer program and a printer or a copy machine, increase or decrease the size of the image. Follow the instructions in the Telamadera Fusion process for transferring images to the SAS2 (see page 15–16).

Cutting trapped spaces

Using the scissors, cut around the image, leaving 1/8" (3mm) beyond the drawn lines. For trapped spaces, gently fold the fabric and make a small snip inside the space.

Finish design

Using the scissors, cut out the trapped spaces. Continue creating the art piece using the Telamadera Fusion process.

Exaggerated Size

Matte photo paper makes it easy to alter a photo by touching it up with colored pencils or adding elements, such as the shoes I added on my daughter's feet with a black fine-tipped permanent marker. You can use fabric elements, such as the small flowers, to hide unwanted parts of photos, too.

FLOWER CHILDREN

In scrapbooking we see how personal photos are given amazing artistic backgrounds. You can use this concept in your artwork by using personal images and altering them for effect and visual interest. This project simply enlarges an image of a sunflower and shrinks an image of my children.

Prepare photo images

Once you have decided how the images will form part of the overall design, incorporate them into the artwork using the Telamadera Fusion process, stopping before adding the varnish (page 19) or any surface embellishments.

Using the photo-editing software of your choice, enlarge or reduce the photos as desired. Print the photos onto the matte photo paper. Using the scissors, cut out the desired images.

To use SAS2 with the images, cut a piece of SAS2 slightly bigger than the image you have chosen. Peel away paper side A and place the SAS2 directly onto the back of the image. Using your fingers, press the SAS2 to the image to temporarily adhere it to the image. Using the scissors, trim the SAS2 as close to the image as possible.

Place the image face down on the ironing surface. Place the scrap cloth over the image. Using the iron on a wool setting, fuse the image to the SAS2.

Fuse picture to background

Let the image cool completely. Gently peel away paper backing side B from the image. Place the photo where you want it on the artwork surface. Place the scrap cloth over the photo. Using the iron on a wool setting, fuse the image to the artwork surface.

Finish the artwork following the rest of the Telamadera Fusion process.

Stencils for Fabric

Decorator stencils are not just for paint but for fabric, too. They help create repeating patterns that can unify artwork. This stencil design uses two fabrics, but you can use many more if you'd like. The cover of a wood photo album can capture a theme for the memories inside.

Materials

black fine-tipped permanent marker

stencil

paper

Steam-A-Seam 2 (SAS2)

scissors

fabrics

iron

BLUEBIRD LOVE

Bluebirds are often in my artwork. After my yellow Lab, Cassius, died, I was on a walk feeling like my sadness might never go away. I stopped to wipe my tears and twenty or so bluebirds suddenly flew out of a tree and crazily flapped around my head. I laughed as my arms waved frantically. They helped lift my sadness then, and they make me smile now. Symbols can personalize your artwork and infuse it with meaning.

Prepare design
Using the black marker, outline the stencil design on the paper. (Note: My stencil has an A stencil and a B stencil. If you have a two-piece stencil, it's important to trace them in order: A first, then B.)

Trace design onto SAS2
Using the black marker, trace the design onto the back of the SAS2. (The stencil I used does not have a right or left side, so I traced the design directly onto the back of the SAS2. Because one vertical half is the mirror image of the other, the design transfers the same.)

Lay out design
Follow the Telamadera Fusion process for preparing the fabric (page 17). Using the scissors, cut out the pieces. Lay the pieces on their corresponding shapes on top of the paper stencil design to help keep them in order.

Transfer pieces
Remove the back paper of the SAS2 for each piece and place them on the artwork surface, making sure the design is the same as you transfer. Fuse the fabric following the Telamadera Fusion process (page 19) and continue the process until you've finished the piece.

 Tip *When laying the pieces onto the painted surface, find the point you consider the middle and work out from there. I concentrated on placing the largest center pieces first, then worked my way out and around.*

Collage Background

A collage background can keep the eye moving easily around the artwork without detracting from the main subject. Here, batiks and earthy fabrics help push back the background. Tissue paper can mellow out intense colors or pop color. Printed white tissue allows you to see the layer beneath while adding another design element.

Materials

scissors	2 medium paint-brushes	transparent acrylic paint
fabrics	wood surface	water
papers	latex gloves	paper towels
tissue papers	small cup	Teflon pressing sheet
heavy gel (gloss)		

SHE TRANSFORMS THE WORLD

This piece reminds me to transform my thoughts to serve my highest self—that part of me that loves without conditions. If we could move beyond boundaries that reinforce the differences that divide us and instead see our similarities, we'd walk this Earth empowering and supporting the differences that make us each beautifully unique.

Prepare and layer fabrics

Using the scissors, cut various strips of fabric in a free-form manner. Using your hands, tear the paper and tissue paper into strips. Using the paintbrush, apply a generous coat of gel on the wood surface. Put on the gloves.

Using the paintbrush, apply a generous layer of gel to the back of a fabric strip. Lay the fabric strip gel side down onto the wood, and apply more gel to the top of the fabric. Using your fingers, press the piece of fabric to remove air pockets and to flatten it to the surface. Reuse any excess gel. Repeat with all of the fabric strips, placing them randomly on the wood surface.

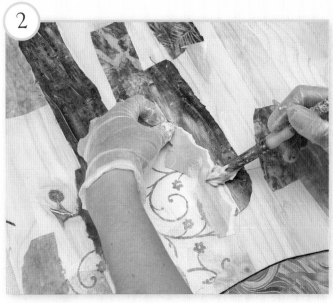

Layer papers

Repeat Step 1, this time using the strips of paper and tissue paper. The papers can overlap the fabric edges, which helps hide any frayed edges.

When layering the tissue paper strips, place them on the gelled surface and very gently slide your fingers over them to adhere them to the background and to remove any air pockets. Use a paintbrush to very lightly apply a layer of the gel to seal the tissue paper to the surface.

Apply paint

When the wood surface has been covered to your liking, let it dry completely.

In the small cup, dilute some transparent acrylic paint with a small amount of water. Using the clean paintbrush, apply the diluted paint to any exposed wood surfaces. (This will help unify the elements of the background.) Using the paper towel, wipe away any excess stain.

Let the background dry completely. Continue with the Telamadera Fusion process, following this very important rule: When ironing on any fabric, use the Teflon sheet between the iron and the fabric to keep the soft gel from melting. You must let the Teflon sheet cool completely before removing it.

Tip

I like to use three to five strips of each piece of fabric, paper and tissue paper I choose. This helps create visual repetition and draws the eye around the piece.

Weaving Metal Leaf and Fabric

Sherrill Kahn, a talented artist who wrote a must-have book called *Creative Embellishments*, details how to weave paper and fabric in her gorgeous collages. With her permission I have added a twist to this technique by backing metallic foil with fusible webbing and weaving it with fabric.

Materials

metal leaf

scissors

Steam-A-Seam 2 (SAS2)

Teflon pressing sheet

ironing board

iron

fabric

I AM THE DROP AND THE OCEAN

I am amazed at the generosity of people who give so much of their time and energy to improve the lives of others. I love that our global community gets smaller daily as we connect with others around the world. It is my hope that we all truly see how our smallest actions ripple like a drop in the ocean and that together we generate waves that change our lives for the better—for everyone and everything, everywhere.

Cut metal leaf package

Open the metal leaf package and gently lift the metal leaf pieces; notice how they each rest on an individual piece of tissue and how they are sewn together at the top. Using the scissors, cut close to the sewn line so you have a stack of metal leaf and tissue. Avoid touching the metal leaf with your hands because it is very fragile and disintegrates easily.

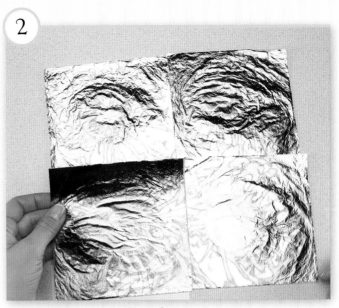

Move sheets to work surface

Remove the protective plastic sheet off the top of the stack of metal leaf. Gently pull the first tissue onto the work surface, minimally touching the metal leaf that sits on top of the tissue. Leave the tissue under the metal leaf. Repeat with three more pieces to form a large square. Slightly overlap the individual metal leaf sheets. You can use more or fewer sheets depending on how large you want the woven metal leaf and fabric to be.

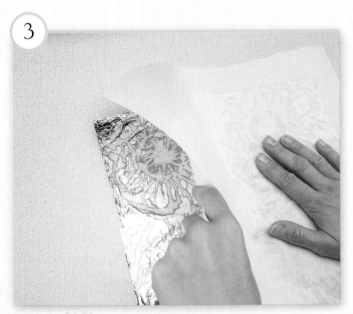

Prepare SAS2

Away from the metal leaf, use the scissors to cut a piece of the SAS2 that is large enough to cover the metal leaf sheets (four in the square configuration). Remove the top paper A to reveal the fusible webbing. Turn the SAS2 over and carefully lay it directly on the metal leaf, covering it completely. Using your hands, gently press the SAS2 so the metal leaf sticks to the SAS2.

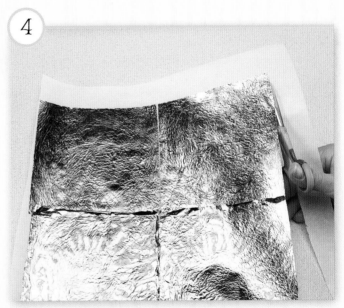

Trim excess SAS2

Carefully turn over the SAS2–metal leaf sheet. Using the scissors, carefully cut away the excess SAS2.

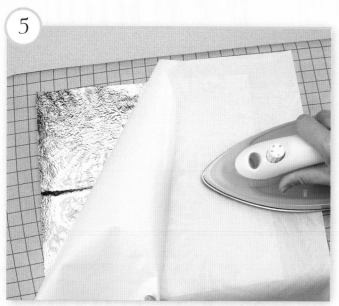

5

Iron sheet

Gently place the metal leaf sheet onto the ironing board. Place the Teflon pressing sheet on top of the metal leaf sheet. Using the iron on the silk setting, iron the Teflon sheet. Do not overheat. (Overheating can cause the color to change, so keep the iron moving.) Do not remove the Teflon sheet until it is completely cool. Test that the gold leaf and SAS2 have fused completely by lifting a corner of the metal leaf. Repeat this step as necessary to fuse the metal leaf and SAS2.

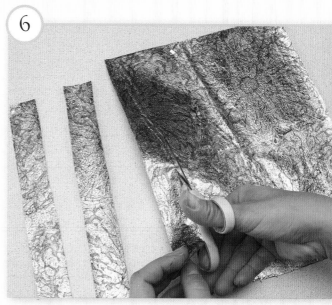

6

Cut strips

Allow the Teflon sheet to cool completely. Gently peel the Teflon sheet away. Gently peel off paper side B of the SAS2. Using the scissors, cut the newly created gold leaf fabric into strips. I cut mine in approximately 1" (3cm) wide strips.

7

Prepare second fabric

Prepare the second piece of fabric the same size as the gold leaf fabric you just made. Follow the Telamadera Fusion instructions for fusing fabric to the SAS2 (see page 17). Using the scissors, cut the fabric into strips the same width as the metallic strips, leaving 1" (3cm) uncut at the top of the sheet.

Tip

If you're having trouble removing the backing from side B, trim a little bit off the edges. This may help to loosen the paper backing at the edge.

Begin weaving fabrics

Remove paper backing B from the fabric. Take one of the gold leaf fabric strips and weave it over and under the other fabric. While you are weaving, carefully push the fabrics together.

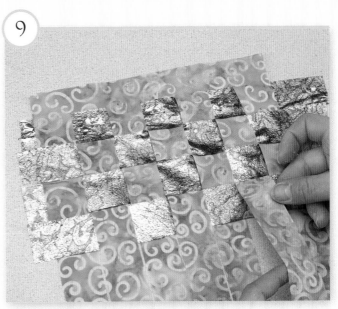

Continue weaving

Using the rest of the metal leaf fabric, continue weaving the fabrics together. A checker pattern should emerge. Carefully push the fabrics together to create a tight weave.

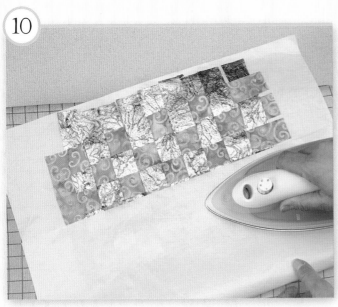

Fuse woven fabric

Lay the Teflon sheet on the ironing board. Lift the woven fabric and place it on top of one half of the Teflon sheet. Fold the Teflon sheet over the top of the woven fabric. Using an iron on the wool setting, iron the Teflon pressing sheet, avoiding the fold. (You do not want to iron a crease into the Teflon sheet.) Let the Teflon sheet cool completely. Gently peel away the woven fabric and repeat this step for the other half of the fabric. Let the fabric cool completely before removing it from the Teflon sheet.

This woven fabric can now be used as a fabric piece in Telamadera Fusion artwork.

Tip

When fusing the weaving to the wood surface, be sure to use the Teflon sheet between the iron and the artwork to fuse it in place. Other fabrics can be fused with the Teflon sheet as well, just use a wool setting because the Teflon gets very hot. Again, let it cool completely before removing it.

Embedding Mirrors

There is something empowering about power tools! Circular drill bits create places in the wood to add Shisha mirrors, which you can find at your local craft store. Try adding mirrors to borders or to a mandala design.

Materials

wood surface

pencil

drill with drill bits in 3 sizes: ¾" (2cm), 1" (3cm) and 1¼" (32mm)

fine grit sandpaper

acrylic paint

paintbrush

Shisha mirrors in 3 sizes: ½" (1cm), ¾" (2cm) and 1" (3cm)

Aleene's 7800 adhesive

REFLECTION ON THE WATER

I am always amazed at how artists are able to paint the reflection of a landscape in water with such realism. Here we create a different reflection that sparkles in its own way. I call it reflective art. When your artwork receives a wonderful comment such as "beautiful," the mirrors reflect that sentiment right back to the viewer.

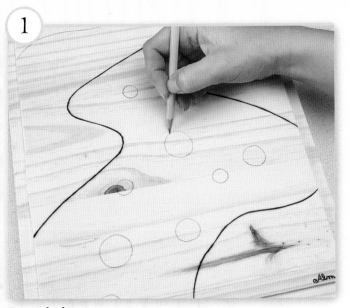

Draw holes

Determine the placement of the mirrors when creating the design. Using the pencil, draw circles on the wood surface where you want the holes to be.

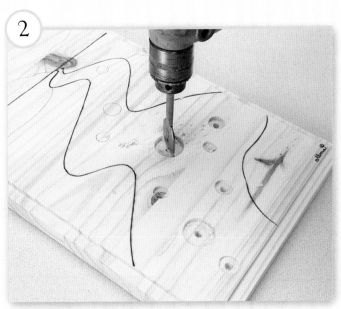

Drill holes

Drill the marked holes using the three drill bits. The holes you create using the various drill bits are slightly larger than the Shisha mirrors. For a ¾" (2cm) hole, use a ½" (1cm) Shisha mirror; pair a 1" (3cm) hole with a ¾" (2cm) mirror; and the 1¼" (32mm) hole will fit a 1" (3cm) Shisha mirror.

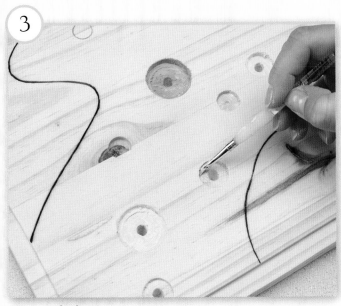

Prepare holes

Using the sandpaper, sand the holes and the edges of each hole until smooth. Using the paintbrush, paint the interior of each hole with the acrylic paint.

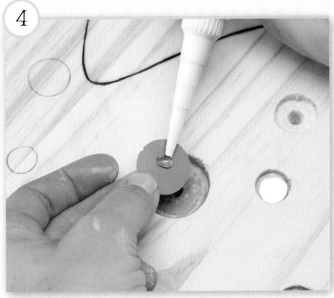

Add mirrors

Let the paint dry completely. Apply the Aleene's 7800 adhesive to the backs of the Shisha mirrors. Gently push the mirrors into place and let them dry. Continue with the Telamadera Fusion process.

Tip

Looking for a little more gloss? Let the paint dry. Using a paintbrush, apply one to two coats of Liquitex High Gloss Varnish. Let the varnish layers dry completely before adding the mirrors.

Sinking Crystals

Sinking items incorporates them into a surface and secures them. After I added Shisha mirrors to the wood in *Reflection on the Water*, I realized I could add all kinds of things. I'm partial to all things shiny and glittery, so I used crystals next. You could also add marbles, bits of glass, colorful rocks or beads.

Materials

- wood surface
- pencil
- drill with 1" (3cm) bit
- fine grit sandpaper
- acrylic paint
- paintbrush
- half crystals (flat bottom) in various sizes
- small tongs to hold crystals (optional)
- Elmer's liquid glue
- Diamond Glaze
- straight pin

BE THE LIGHT

"When you possess light within, you see it externally."
—Anaïs Nin

I say we are all beams of light, but sometimes we forget to turn the light switch on! When we do remember, we can help bring others out of the darkness.

Prepare background and place crystals

Refer to Step 1 of *Embedding Mirrors* (page 47) to determine the placement of the crystals when you create the design. Refer to Step 2 of *Embedding Mirrors* (page 47), use the drill and the 1" (3cm) bit to make the holes.

Using the sandpaper, sand inside and around the edges of each hole until smooth. Paint and add fabric layers on the background using the Telamadera Fusion process (pages 14–20).

When you're satisfied with the background, use the paintbrush and acrylic paint to paint the inside of the holes. Let the paint dry completely. Holding each crystal with the tongs, apply a small amount of liquid glue to the back and place it in the hole. Repeat for all crystals, arranging them to your liking.

Add Diamond Glaze

Let the glue dry completely. Pour the Diamond Glaze into the hole, just covering the crystals. Use the pin to pop any bubbles that form. Repeat this for all the holes.

Allow the Diamond Glaze to dry completely, about 24 hours. (The Diamond Glaze becomes clear when it is completely dry.) Continue with the Telamadera Fusion process.

Dimensional Paint

3-dimensional paint is clean and easy to use. It is the last thing to add before varnishing, and it cannot be ironed. Use the paint to create relief and texture on your artwork.

Materials

fabric pencil

scrap paper

dimensional paint

straight pin

WEAVE YOUR WEB

"The means to gain happiness is to throw out from oneself like a spider in all directions an adhesive web of love, and to catch in it all that comes."

—Leo Tolstoy

The spider has long been a symbol for creation. Her web is a metaphor for weaving our own experiences. What inspirations are you weaving? What dreams will you catch in your web?

Draw design

Create a Telamadera Fusion piece (pages 14–19), but do not varnish it yet. Using the fabric pencil, lightly outline a design on the fabric.

Apply dimensional paint

Apply the dimensional paint to the surface. Use the straight pin to unclog the tip of the bottle should it become clogged and to pop any air bubbles that form on the artwork. Let the dimensional paint dry completely, about 1 to 2 hours, before beginning the varnish process.

Tip

A new bottle of dimensional paint has air in it at the top. You should remove as much air as you can before applying it to the artwork. With the lid on the dimensional paint bottle, shake the bottle, tip down. Remove the lid and give the bottle a couple more shakes, tip down, in the direction of the scrap paper. Squeeze a very small amount onto the scrap paper to make sure there are no air bubbles.

Tip

The bumpier surface created by the dimensional paint will naturally create more bubbles when varnishing. Blowing on the bubbles will help get rid of them.

The varnish will pool in spaces where the dimensional paint has closed an area. Don't worry, it will dry! Don't brush over the varnish even though you feel inclined to do so, as this could fog the varnish.

Tip

You can apply the dimensional paint directly onto the piece without first drawing a design, but the fabric pencil will give you an opportunity to make changes. Be sure to make light marks, and use the fabric pencil eraser sparingly. Consider practicing on a piece of scrap paper first.

Plaster

Ordinary plaster of paris, which you can find at your local hardware store, works great for this technique. I love how the rough, matte look of plaster contrasts with the smooth, glossy finish of the Telamadera Fusion. Gather all your supplies before you begin and determine the placement, because the plaster of paris dries quickly.

Materials

plaster of paris

water

plastic container

spatula or palette knife

breathing mask

acrylic paint in metallic gold (optional)

plastic gloves

elements to embed in plaster

paintbrush

glitter (optional)

paper towels

MOTHER AND CHILD

On our way to a hike in Maui, I found beautiful aqua-colored broken car window glass along a road. I marveled at how the glass matched the color of the shallow water offshore below. I had to have it! There are so many things you can embed in plaster like small tiles, rocks, branches and buttons. What treasures will you incorporate?

1

Prepare design

Create the artwork using the Telamadera Fusion process (pages 14–19), stopping before varnishing. Plan the design to determine where you will add the plaster.

Using the glass pieces, shells and any other desired items, lay out the design.

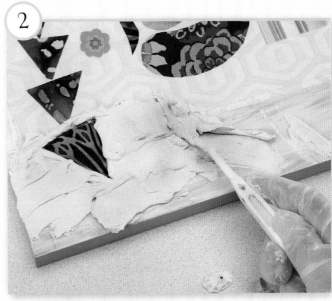

2

Mix and apply plaster

Wearing the gloves and the breathing mask, follow the manufacturer's directions for mixing the plaster in the plastic container. Using the spatula or palette knife, spread the plaster onto the background as if you were frosting a cake, leaving peaks and valleys if that is your desired effect.

3

Place design

Working quickly, embed the design you laid out in Step 1. Use the spatula or palette knife to build up the plaster around the larger elements, such as the shells. Use the handle of the paintbrush to push the elements into the plaster.

4

Paint plaster (optional)

While the plaster is still wet, use the paintbrush and metallic gold acrylic paint to decorate the plaster.

5

Apply glitter

While the plaster is still wet, pour some glitter into your palm. Using your fingers, pinch a small amount of glitter and sprinkle it on the desired areas of plaster. Gently press the glitter into the surface. (You will lose some glitter.)

Using the paper towel, quickly clean the edges of the wood, being careful not to break plaster pieces from the surface. Let the plaster dry completely before continuing with the Telamadera Fusion process. I did not varnish the plaster for this piece, but it can be done.

Tip *Plaster of paris dries very quickly, so your working time is short. Before you mix the plaster, decide what pieces of fabric you want to cover or keep uncovered. For this piece, I covered a small portion of fabric with plaster and then spread the plaster around a piece of fabric (seen at the bottom of the palm tree).*

Tip *Have the container of glass bits close by in case you need to add or swap pieces.*

Angelina Fibers

I took a leap of faith when deciding to use Angelina fibers with Telamadera Fusion. It comes in fantastic, wispy, iridescent colors that I have enjoyed using in art quilts, but I wasn't sure how it would look under several coats of varnish. It turns out that I like it, and I hope you do, too. I recommend a few coats of varnish on the Angelina fibers (I applied four), assessing whether more is needed as you go. I applied ten coats on the rest of the piece.

Materials

Angelina fibers	scissors	craft knife
black fine-tipped permanent marker	fabric	glue stick
Steam-A-Seam 2 (SAS2)	Teflon pressing sheet	scrap fabric
	iron	

ANGEL

"It is only with the heart that one can see rightly; what is essential is invisible to the eye."

—Antoine de Saint-Exupery

Angel *celebrates our ability to hold each other so we don't fall.*

Place SAS2 onto background

To begin, determine what part of your design will have the Angelina fibers on it. Using the marker, trace this design onto paper side A of the SAS2. Using the scissors, cut the SAS2 on the drawn lines. Remove paper A and place the SAS2, fusible webbing side down, onto the background. Carefully remove paper side B without tearing the webbing. The fusible webbing is now exposed on the surface.

Apply Angelina fibers

Consult the design and place any additional fabric elements (backed with SAS2) that will be underneath the Angelina fibers first. Apply the Angelina fibers to completely cover the fusible webbing, staying within the piece of SAS2.

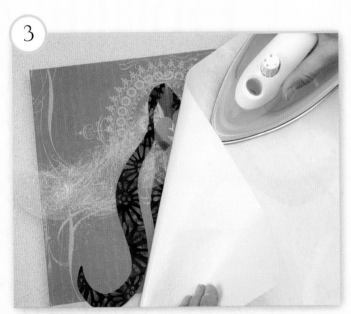

Iron fibers

At this time, apply any of the fabric elements that surround or go on top of the Angelina fibers. Place the Teflon pressing sheet on top of the Angelina fibers and the other fabric elements. Using the iron on a wool setting, iron over the Teflon sheet. Keep the iron moving because the fibers will quickly adhere to themselves and to the SAS2.

Trim stray fibers

Using the scissors, trim off any stray Angelina fibers.

5

Apply glue

Using the craft knife, dig a small chunk of glue out of the glue stick. Apply small pieces of glue stick to various places directly on the Angelina fibers.

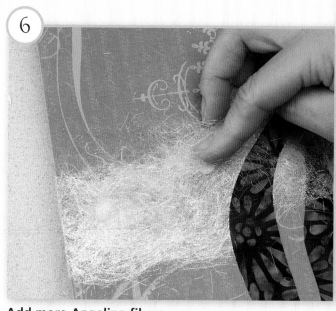

6

Add more Angelina fibers

Add more fibers to the surface, pushing them into the pieces of glue. Allow the glue to dry completely before varnishing.

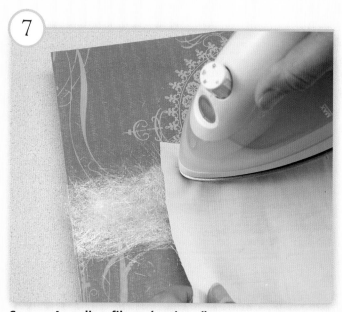

7

Secure Angelina fibers (optional)

Place the piece of scrap fabric loosely on top of the Angelina fibers. Using only the tip of the iron, fuse tiny areas of the top fibers to the first layer. Try to keep some Angelina fibers loose on the surface. The varnish process will collapse some of these loose fibers, but allows for some texture on the surface.

Tip

As you add more fabric pieces to the artwork, keep the iron away from the Angelina fibers. If you must get close to the fibers, use the tip of the iron.

When varnishing with the Liquitex High Gloss Varnish, brush the varnish onto the Angelina fibers generously but with a light touch so as not to collapse the fibers too much. Avoid overbrushing. Blow on any bubbles, too. The rest of the artwork is varnished using a thinner coat than you used for the Angelina fibers.

Curved Surface

You can add all kinds of things to gourds—old keys, chimes and ribbons are just a few options. I found mine cut and pre-cleaned, so all I had to do was drill a hole on the tops and dress them up.

Materials

hollow, clean gourd

drill with ⅛" (3mm) bit (Dremel tool works well)

saw

breathing mask

acrylic paints

mini-iron

Steam-A-Seam 2 (SAS2)

scrap cloth (optional)

water

plastic container

paintbrush

scissors

fabric

leather cord, chain or rope

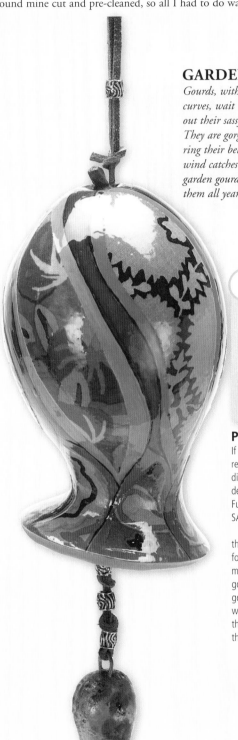

GARDEN GOURD

Gourds, with their plain color and soft curves, wait unassumingly for you to bring out their sassy dispositions and full figures. They are gorgeous all dressed up, ready to ring their bells and sway their curves as the wind catches beneath them. I like to hang my garden gourds inside by the window to enjoy them all year long.

Prepare gourd

If the gourd still has a stem, use the small saw to remove it. Using the drill and the 1/8" (3mm) bit, drill directly into the stem or just next to it. Prepare the design and the fabric as you would for any Telamadera Fusion piece (pages 14–19), backing the fabric with SAS2.

Apply the fabrics to their coordinating spaces on the gourd. If needed, use the scissors to trim the fabrics for a better fit. Wearing the breathing mask, use the mini-iron on the high setting to fuse the fabric to the gourd. Keep moving the iron around all the areas of the gourd until the fabrics have fused completely. Contours will take longer to fuse. When using any fabric other than cotton, use a scrap cloth between the surface and the mini-iron

Paint inside of gourd

In the plastic container, dilute the acrylic paint with water. Using the paintbrush, paint the inside of the gourd.

Allow the paint to dry completely. Complete the gourd using the Telamadera Fusion process. If you want to hang the gourd outside, add two coats of exterior water-based varnish after the ten coats of Liquitex varnish. This will help protect the beautiful designs from the elements.

When you've finished the varnishing process, thread leather cord, chain or rope through the hole drilled in Step 1, knotting the material to hold the gourd. Embellish the cord with beads, bells or whatever you would like.

> **Tip** *Drawing the design from the gourd to the SAS2 does not guarantee that the fabric shape will fit precisely in the area on the gourd. The proper fit will depend on how curvy the gourd is. You may have to trim the fabric to better fit the contours of the gourd.*

Adding Metal and Mini-Quilt

A simple house design with a little quilt on a clothing line reminds me of days gone by. This technique gives a scrap quilt new meaning as the smallest bits of fabrics are used without any sewing. This is a fun project to create your first art quilt for.

Materials

ruler or straightedge

black permanent marker

galvanized metal flashing

metal shears

fine grit sandpaper

Steam-A-Seam 2 (SAS2)

iron

hammer

sharp nail

copper-plated canvas tacks or #4 aluminum cut tacks

dimensional paint (optional)

beads

embroidery floss

embroidery needle

paper

pencil

fabrics

scrap fabric

mini wooden clothespin

scissors

LITTLE HOUSE

When I first began quilting, Freddy Moran, author of Freddy's House: Brilliant Color in Quilts, *inspired me to be playful with color. Her book gave me permission to boldly paint my home and to live creatively. I liked what Freddy had to say, loved her big red-rimmed glasses and loved her quilts more. I thought of her as I designed* Little House.

Metal Roof

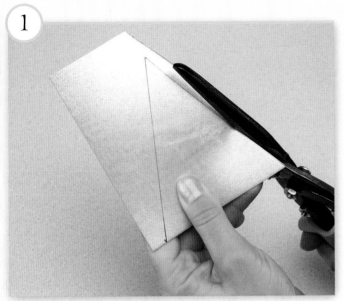

Prepare triangle

Create an art piece following the Telamadera Fusion process (pages 14–19). Complete this techniques after all coats of the varnish have dried.

Determine the size of the triangle. Using a ruler or straightedge and the marker, draw the triangle onto the metal flashing. Using the metal shears, cut out the triangle shape.

2

Begin holes

Using the sandpaper, sand the edges of the metal. If desired, prepare and apply any SAS2 circles and iron them on. Let the metal cool completely before moving it. Using the hammer and the sharp nail, hammer three holes close to each tip of the triangle (a few easy taps) to begin a hole for the copper canvas nails.

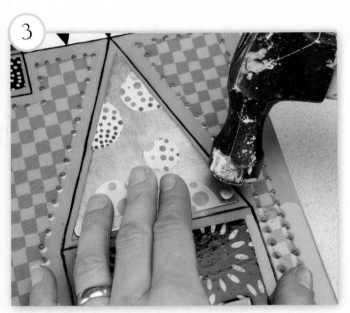

3

Add copper nails

Using the hammer, gently hammer the copper nails into the holes prepared in Step 2.

Add string

If desired, embellish the circle shapes with dimensional paint. Tie a bead to the end of the embroidery floss. Tie the piece of embroidery floss to the copper canvas nail. Attach the other end of the embroidery floss to the back of the art piece by securing it with another copper nail. Make sure the floss is taut.

5

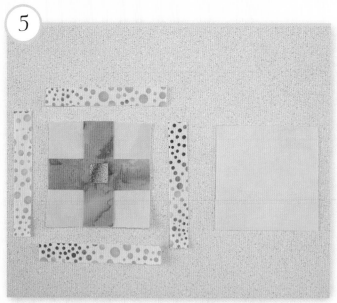

Prepare mini-quilt
This is a sawtooth star design. You may use this design or create your own. On the paper, draw out the quilt design. The entire example quilt measures 3" × 3" (8cm × 8cm) and is made up of a plain backing square, a front designed square and four side strips. All the pieces are backed with SAS2.

6

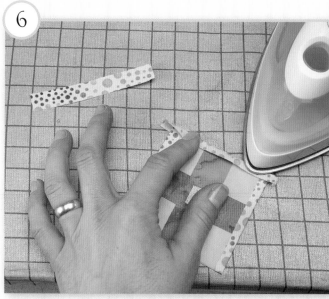

Begin assembling mini-quilt
Bring the backing fabric and the front fabric SAS2 sides together. Place the scrap piece of cotton over the fabric pieces. Using the iron on a wool setting, fuse the fabrics.

Take one side strip and fold it evenly over one edge of the square. Using the iron, fuse the side strip to the main quilt piece. Using the scissors, trim off any excess fabric hanging over the square. Repeat for the other side strips.

7

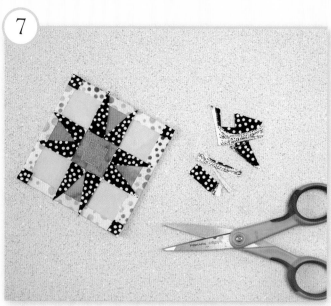

Finish mini-quilt
Using the scissors, cut out the SAS2-backed triangle shapes. Using the iron, fuse the triangle shapes to the front of the mini-quilt. (I overlapped the triangles onto the border.) Add small squares to the corners in the same fashion.

8

Hang mini-quilt
If desired, embellish the mini-quilt with the dimensional paint. Using the mini clothespin, secure the mini-quilt to the embroidery floss.

Adding Craft Wood Pieces

Small, flat wood craft pieces are sold in a variety of shapes and sizes. In artwork they create relief and texture and serve as mini-canvases, too (check out *Flowers and Hearts* on page 74). They can help you emphasize form in your artwork. Here the circle shapes I used for *Garden Party* reinforce the fabric patterns I used and the circle shapes I wood burned.

Prepare craft wood

Create a complete Telamadera art piece (pages 14–19). Apply Telamadera Fusion process to the craft wood pieces by painting them, adding fabric to them and varnishing them. Let them dry thoroughly. Apply the adhesive to the back of the craft wood pieces.

Add craft wood to art piece

Apply the craft wood pieces directly to the varnished surface of the artwork. Immediately remove any adhesive strands. Let the glue dry completely before handling the artwork.

GARDEN PARTY

Between the deer that call our yard home and the long winter season, I don't have an opportunity to plant many flowers. With artwork I can invent my own varieties and clothe them in fun fabric patterns. More importantly, they cheer me up during the long winter months.

Materials

circular craft wood pieces of various sizes

Aleene's 7800 adhesive

Designing With a Small Quilt

Quilts are beautiful hung on walls, but you can set off a small one by creating a glossy surface with contrast between the background and the foreground. Center your quilt to make it the focal point or move it to the side, bringing the design of the Telamadera Fusion piece into your quilt. Add your quilt when the varnishing process is complete.

Materials

- ⅜" (9mm) dowel
- fine grit sandpaper
- Two 1" (3cm) wood cubes
- carbon paper
- pencil
- scrap wood
- small clamps

- drill with ½" (1cm) drill bit
- wood glue or Aleene's 7800 adhesive
- paper towel
- fabrics
- scissors
- ¼ yard (¼m) Steam-A-Seam 2 (SAS2)

- iron
- small piece of lightweight interfacing
- dimensional paint
- beads for embellishment
- embroidery floss
- embroidery needle

TREE FAIRY

The forest where I live seems quiet, but tree fairies disguise themselves as creatures and events that make our walks exciting. They push pinecones from trees, barely missing us, or they shake snow from branches onto our dog, Augustus, who runs away excitedly. Sometimes they are squirrels darting into hollowed logs and enticing Augustus to play hide-and-seek. Thankfully he never wins.

1

Prepare wood pieces

This technique is employed at the very beginning and the very end of the Telamadera Fusion process. Create an art piece following the Telamadera Fusion process (pages 14–19). When drawing the design, you should incorporate the quilt design into the overall piece. Make sure the design fits the dimensions of the wood. Remember to allow space for the wood cubes and dowel the quilt will hang from.

If needed, cut the dowel to the desired length using your favorite method. Using the sandpaper, smooth any rough edges or patches on the dowel and the wood cubes.

Using the pencil, mark the center of the wood cube. Place the wood cube onto the piece of scrap wood. Using the clamp, secure the wood cube and scrap wood to a sturdy surface. Using the ½" (1cm) drill bit, drill one hole into the wood cube that goes through the other end.

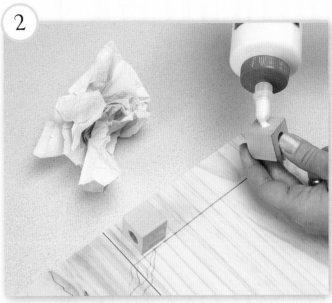

2

Attach wood pieces

Using the carbon paper and pencil, transfer the design you created in Step 1 to the wood background. Using the wood glue, adhere the wood cube to the background wood so the holes in each cube line up. Using a paper towel, wipe away any excess glue. Repeat Steps 1 and 2 for the second wood cube.

Continue creating the piece following the Telamadera Fusion process, including painting and varnishing the wood blocks and the dowel. (The dowel only needs one coat of varnish.) Allow the dowel to dry separately and thoroughly before attaching it to the main piece.

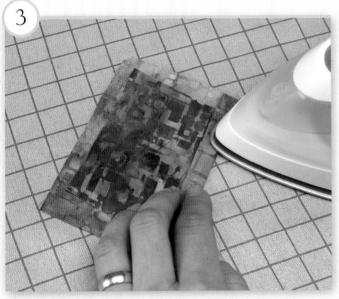

3

Begin quilt

To make the quilt sleeve, first determine the size you would like it to be. In my example I used two pieces of fabric with SAS2 between them and fused them together. One piece should be at least ¼" (6mm) wider on each vertical edge and backed with SAS2. Place the large piece, fusible side down, on the back of a smaller piece of fabric. Fold the ¼" (6mm) edges over the smaller fabric. Using the iron on a cotton setting, fuse the fabrics together. This provides a clean edge without sewing.

4

Layer quilt

This quilt consists of plain backing fabric and a layered front panel, all backed with SAS2, along with the piece of interfacing that is the same size as the backing fabric and the sleeve from Step 3.

Create a quilt sandwich in this manner: Place the backing fabric, SAS2 side up, on the ironing surface. Place the sleeve from Step 3 right side down at the top of the backing fabric so one of the raw edges overlaps the backing fabric by ½" (1cm). Place the interfacing over the backing fabric and the sleeve edge. Carefully flip the sandwich so the right side of the backing fabric faces up. Using the iron, fuse the layers together.

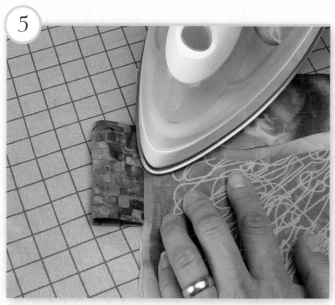

5

Finish layers

Allow the backing layers to cool. Flip the piece so the interfacing is on top again. Finish layering the quilt in the following fashion: Place the front fabric on top of the interfacing. Fold the sleeve in half and tuck the remaining raw edge between the top fabric and the interfacing so at least ½" (1cm) of the raw edge is hidden between the layers. Using the iron, fuse the layers together.

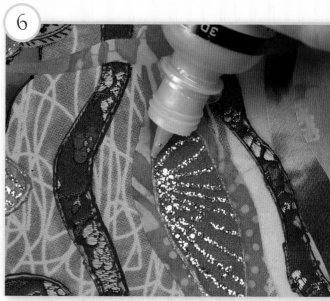

6

Embellish quilt

Continue fusing fabrics to the quilt to complete the design. If desired, embellish the quilt by sewing on beads and using dimensional paint.

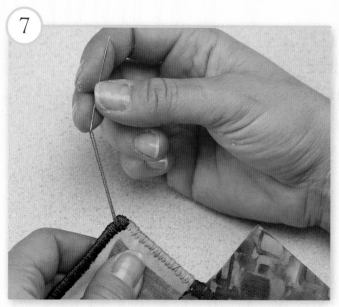

7

Finish quilt edges

Using the embroidery thread and needle, sew the raw edges of the quilt. Sew over the sleeve to reinforce it.

8

Attach quilt to art piece

After all ten coats of varnish have been applied and have dried, add the quilt by running the dowel through the first cube. Hang the quilt on the dowel, then run the dowel through the hole of the other wood cube.

Tip *If you need to walk away from the project for a while before fusing all the fabric layers together in step 5, use straight pins to secure the fabric loop to the project.*

Gallery

LISTEN TO YOUR HEART
Metal and 3-D paint

WHAT WE CREATE
Fabric and paper collage, Shisha mirrors and 3-D paint

SECRET GARDEN
Transparent paints and 3-D paint

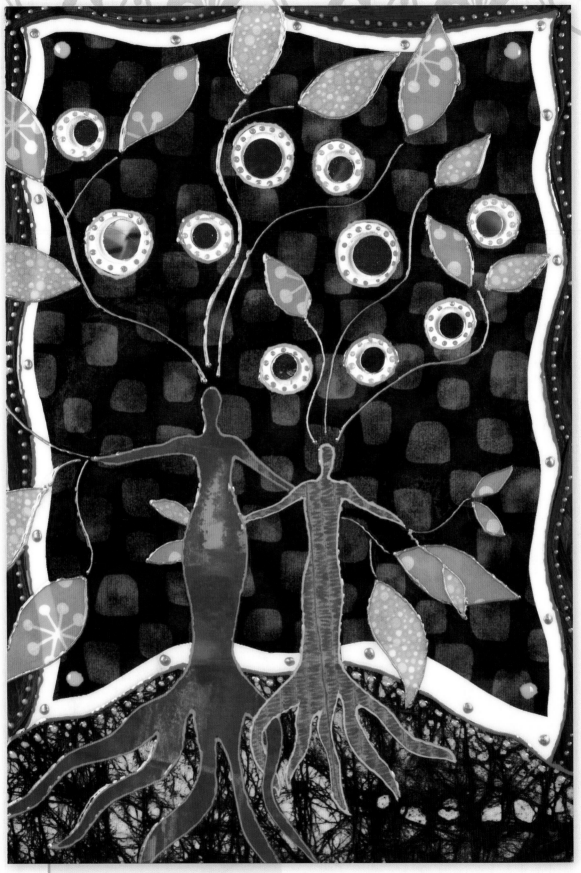

NEW GROWTH
Shisha mirrors and 3-D paint

GOURDGEOUS BELLS
Telamadera Fusion on curvy gourds

SPRING BOUNTY
Transparent paints and 3-D paint

If dandelions make dreams come true,
I'll grow a field of them
and wait for you.

DANDELION WISHES

Images with exaggerated size and Transparent paint

Projects

"An empty canvas is full."
—Robert Rauschenberg

If our eyes are the windows to our soul then our eyes draw us toward what our soul inherently knows it wants. Everything we are drawn to invites us to explore another aspect of ourselves. And so it is with Telamadera Fusion: The basic technique can be mixed with your favorite artistic processes.

The following projects experiment with crossover from one field of expression to another. Beading combines with canvas in *Balance* (page 90); scrapbooking supplies make their way into a wall hanging in *Home* (page 98); and fabric works mix with encaustic in *Listen* (page 84)—all with the Telamadera Fusion technique as a starting point. Walking around your home or going to a fabric, hardware, scrapbooking, craft or art supply store provide opportunities to see how supplies can be combined in ways that speak to you.

As you follow these projects, see what other possibilities are lying around. Sometimes my studio floor speaks the loudest as scraps of supplies layer themselves in new combinations that urge me to take a closer look at those happy accidents.

Detail of *Sacred Spaces*

FLOWERS AND HEARTS

When working this small, I like to pretend the canvas is big, dividing the plane into sections. Don't let size keep you from creating a background and foreground. Off-center focal points attract the eye to what is happening in the rest of the piece. Consider alternatives to jewelry chains for hanging your pendant, for instance satin cords, leather, ribbon, fancy yarns and fabric strips.

Flowers and Hearts
Jewelry

Be warned, these are highly addictive projects. Save your tiniest pieces of fabric from other projects to create one-of-a-kind jewelry. Sometimes less is more, but other times more is more! You might have a collection of jewelry findings already, or you may be inspired to go on a treasure hunt.

 Materials

HEARTS

scissors

satin cording

tube finding

needle-nose pliers

silver clasp

fine grit sandpaper

1" × 2" (3cm × 5cm) rectangular craft wood

transparent acrylic paint in dark green

water

paintbrush

green embroidery floss

crystal or bead

craft knife

glue stick

4" (10cm) ribbon, ½" (1cm) wide

4 small fabrics

Steam-A-Seam 2 (SAS2)

fine-tipped permanent marker

scrap cloth

iron

dimensional paint in Crystal Gel Sparkle, light green and gold

pink half crystal (plastic)

FLOWERS

2" (5cm) diameter craft wood circle, ¼" (6mm) thick

scrap wood

drill with ⅛" (3mm) bit

paintbrush

acrylic paint in gold

5 small fabrics

1 piece of glitter paper

Steam-A-Seam 2 (SAS2)

fine-tipped permanent marker

pencil

scissors

scrap fabric

iron

green satin cording

wire cutters

copper wire

assorted jump rings in faux gold, brass, silver and copper finishes

gold clasp

dimensional paint in copper, gold and light purple

heart charm

needle-nose pliers

Flowers

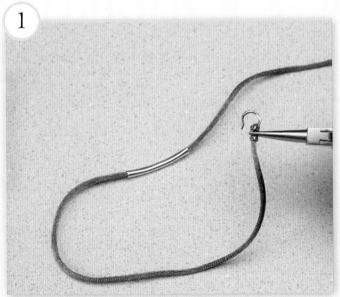

① Prepare cording

Using the scissors, cut the satin cord to the desired length. Run the piece of satin cord through the tube finding. Using the needle-nose pliers, attach the silver clasp to the ends of the cording by squeezing shut the open end of the clasp.

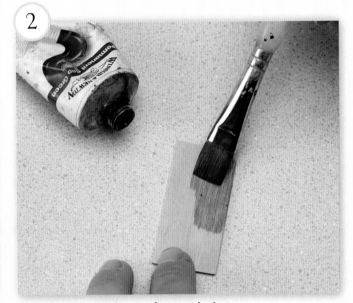

② Prepare retangular craft wood piece

Using the sandpaper, lightly sand the rectangular craft wood piece. Dilute a small amount of the acrylic paint with a little water. Using the paintbrush, brush the watered-down paint evenly onto the front and back of the wood. Let the paint dry completely.

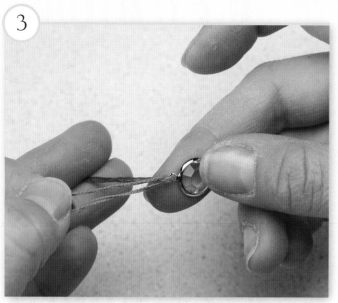

Prepare dangle

Using the scissors, cut a 2" (5cm) piece of the embroidery floss. String the crystal or bead onto the embroidery floss. Tie a knot to secure the bead or crystal, leaving a 1" (3cm) tail.

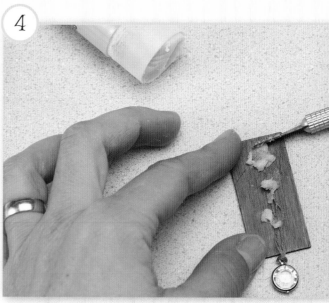

Adhere dangle to craft wood

Place the craft wood face down. Using the craft knife, apply a small piece of glue stick to the back of the craft wood piece. Press the embroidery floss into the glue, allowing the dangle to hang below the wood's edge. Using the craft knife, apply another small piece of glue stick to the upper part of the wood.

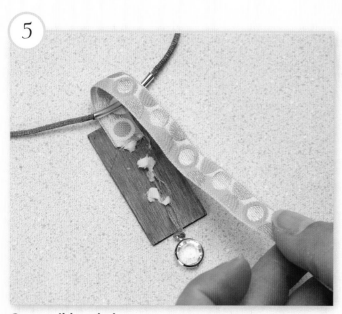

Create ribbon bale

Using the scissors, cut a 3" (8cm) length of the ribbon. With the wrong side (undecorated) of the ribbon facing up, press about a ¼" (6mm) piece of the ribbon into the glue at the top of the craft wood. Loop the ribbon over, creating a ½" (5cm) ribbon bale, large enough for the satin cording to fit through. The right side (decorated) should now be facing you. Add more glue stick as necessary to secure the ribbon to the back of the wood. Press the ribbon into the glue, making sure the ribbon covers the embroidery floss. Using the scissors, trim off the excess ribbon.

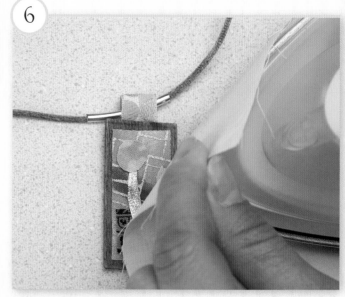

Adhere fabric design

Prepare the fabric pieces as you would in the Telamadera Fusion process (see page 17). Arrange the fabric pieces to your liking on the front of the craft wood. Remove the paper backing from the fabric pieces. Place the scrap cloth over the fabric design. Using the iron on a cotton setting, fuse the fabric to the wood. (For metallic fabric, set the iron to the wool setting.)

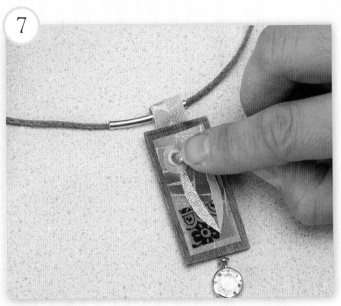

7

Add crystal

Let the piece cool. Place a small amount of the Crystal Gel Sparkle dimensional paint in the center of the flower. Gently push the pink half-crystal into the dimensional paint.

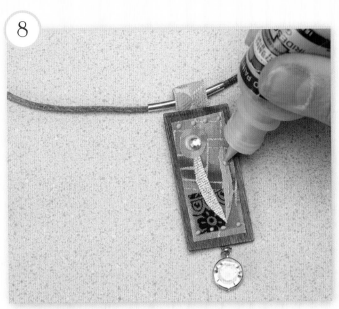

8

Embellish pendant

Using the dimensional paints, embellish the pendant.

Let the pendant dry completely (about an hour). Varnishing is optional. I varnished this piece with the standard ten coats.

Hearts

1

Prepare craft wood disk

Place the craft wood disk onto the piece of scrap wood. Using the drill with a ⅛" (3mm) bit, drill two holes, one on one side, then another directly across from the first hole. These holes are on the top and bottom of the pendant.

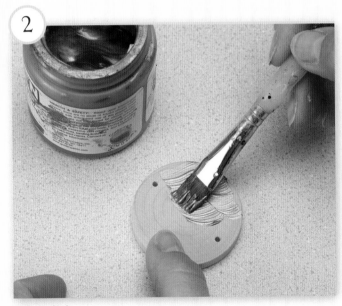

2

Paint disk

Using the paintbrush, paint the front, back and sides of the wood disk with the gold acrylic paint.

Prepare fabric pieces

Prepare the fabric shapes as you would for any other Telamadera Fusion project (see pages 17–18).

Arrange the fabric pieces to your liking on the wood surface. To place the bottom fabric piece (largest pink heart), determine where the bottom hole is. Using the pencil, mark the hole on the heart with a dot.

Adhere fabric

Using the scissors, snip a tiny hole in the largest pink heart. (It helps to fold the fabric a little.) Place the fabric piece on the wood disk, with the fabric hole over the drilled hole. Place the scrap cloth over the pendant. Using the iron on a wool setting, iron the scrap cloth to fuse the fabric.

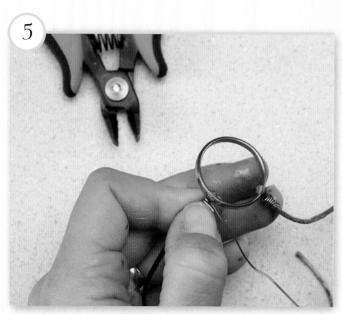

Attach satin cording

Using the scissors, trim two pieces of the satin cording to the length you desire. Using the wire cutters, trim two 2" (5cm) pieces of the copper wire.

To connect the satin cording to the largest jump ring, loop the end of a piece of satin cording once around the large ring. Tightly wrap one of the copper wire pieces around the satin cording, securing the edge of the loop. Repeat for the other piece of satin cording.

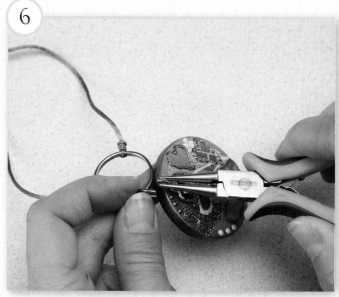

Assemble necklace

Attach the gold clasp to the ends of the satin cord using the wire wrapping method described in Step 5.

Using the dimensional paints, embellish the pendant. Let it dry completely.

Open the jump ring by grasping it with both hands on both sides of the opening. Keeping one hand stationary, twist the other hand away from you. Do not pull the opening apart as that will deform and weaken the jump ring.

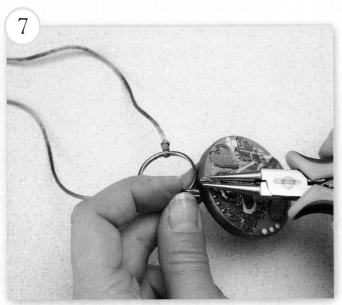

7

Close jump ring

Thread the open jump ring through the hole at the top of the pendant. Slide the large ring and the heart charm onto the open jump ring.

Using the needle-nose pliers and your fingers, close the jump ring by sliding one end to the other in a scissor fashion.

8

Attach bottom dangle

Create the bottom dangle by connecting the metal loops and the heart findings. Connect the dangle to the pendant by gently pushing the hoop through the hole in the wood. Attach the bottom dangle by closing the jump ring as directed in Step 7.

Detail

Emerging
Crackle

My inspiration for this piece came from an armoire that showed its age with peeling, crackled paint. Always with fabric on the brain, I started scheming ways I could use crackle with the Telamadera Fusion process. A canvas turned out to be the perfect background for this lovely lady.

Materials

18" × 24" (46cm × 61cm) canvas

acrylic paint in metallic gray, white and black

medium paintbrush

silver glitter

paper

fine-tipped permanent marker

4 metallic fabrics

red cotton fabric

Steam-A-Seam 2 (SAS2)

heavy book that is at least as big as the iron and as high as the canvas

scrap cloth

iron

crackle medium

dimensional paint in silver glitter and Crystal Gel Sparkle

ruler

Phillips-head screwdriver

2 D-rings with mounting brackets

screws that fit the D-rings

6.2mm picture hanging wire

wire cutters

EMERGING

She might have fallen between the cracks, but art stepped in and showed her a creative world that she holds in her hands and molds to her liking. She emerged without fear or hesitation brighter than she had been before.

1

Paint canvas
Using the paintbrush, paint the entire canvas with the metallic gray acrylic paint.

2

Add glitter
While the paint is still wet, sprinkle silver glitter on the surface. Let the paint dry thoroughly.

3

Create design

Using the black marker and paper, create a design with lots of space for the crackle medium. Number the shapes you draw. (This design has a gray line at the bottom where I did not use the crackle. The gray you see is the metallic gray of the background I painted first in Step 1.)

4

Prepare canvas

Prepare the fabrics for the design according to the Telamadera Fusion process (see pages 17–18). Arrange the fabric pieces onto the canvas.

Place the book under the canvas to act as a hard surface you can iron against. If you don't use a book, be careful not to warp the canvas by pressing the iron against it.

5

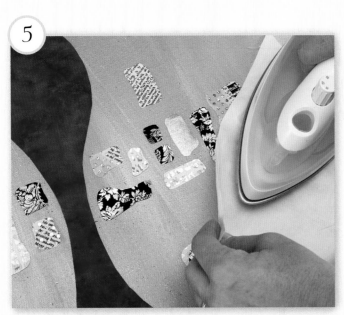

Fuse fabrics to canvas

Place the scrap cloth over the fabric pieces on the canvas. Using the iron (wool setting for metallic fabrics, cotton setting for cotton fabrics), fuse the fabric to the canvas. Move the book and scrap cloth as needed.

6

Apply crackle

Follow the manufacturer's directions to prepare the crackle medium. Using the paintbrush, apply the crackle medium to the entire canvas. Be sure to go around all the fabric pieces.

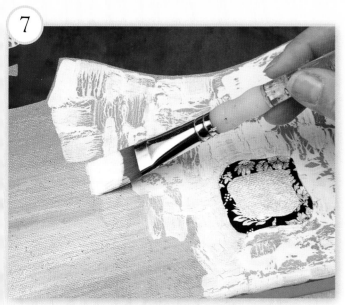

7

Apply paint to tacky crackle

When the crackle becomes tacky (don't wait until it's dry), use the paintbrush to apply the white acrylic paint over all the crackle medium. A generous amount of paint will create deeper cracks.

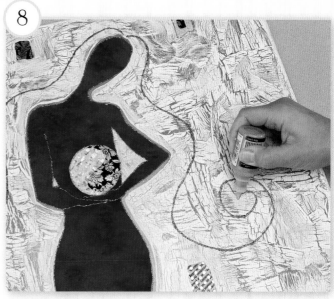

8

Embellish artwork

Let the paint and crackle dry completely. Using the dimensional paint, embellish the artwork.

Let the dimensional paint dry. To finish, paint the sides of the canvas black. Add the hardware (see Steps 15–16 on pages 19–20) to the wood sides on the back of the canvas.

Tip

It is important that the surface of the crackle be tacky to the touch when you spread the acrylic paint. I live in a dry climate so I anticipated having a faster drying time, but those who live in more humid climates might have a longer wait. To be sure, you can test the drying time of the crackle on a small canvas.

Detail

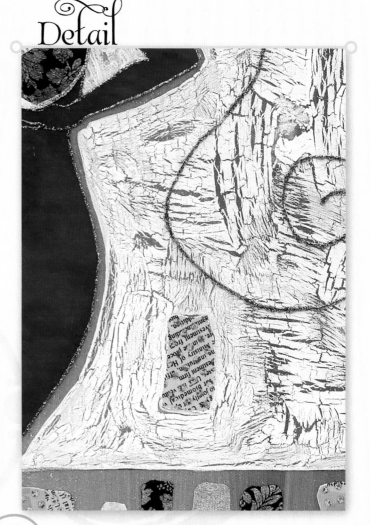

Listen
Encaustic

I love encaustic for its dense translucency, its rich history and its organic quality. It beautifully preserves materials layered within it and, best of all, it's fun. If you have never tried it before, I highly encourage you to do so. A few inexpensive materials are all you need to get started. Work in a well-ventilated area.

Materials

- 12" × 12" (30cm × 30cm) store-bought particleboard craft frame photo window
- hammer
- pencil
- ruler
- 56" (142cm) linear feet of approx. 1½" × ½" (4cm × 1cm) wood trim
- saw
- miter box (optional)
- fine grit sandpaper
- wood glue
- 2 small wood clamps
- paper towels
- art doll face molds
- paper clay
- paintbrush
- metallic acrylic paint
- wood burning tool with universal tip (optional)
- fabrics
- Steam-A-Seam 2 (SAS2)
- fine-tipped permanent marker
- scrap cloth
- iron
- electric hot plate
- clear encaustic medium (wax)
- 2 clean tuna fish or other cans of a similar size
- encaustic tacking iron or small craft iron without steam holes
- encaustic paints in light blue, turquoise, green and white
- craft sticks
- scrapbook paper
- scissors
- white encaustic medium (104ml)
- old credit card
- oven mitt
- small piece of copper sheeting (optional)
- metal shears (optional)
- glitter

LISTEN
Listen to the creative wanderings of your soul.

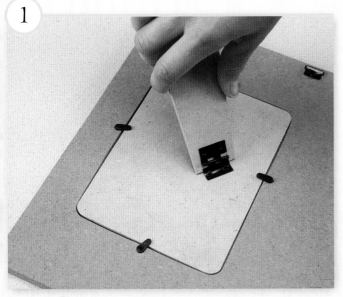

1

Prepare frame
Using your hands, gently pry off the leaning piece from the back of the frame.

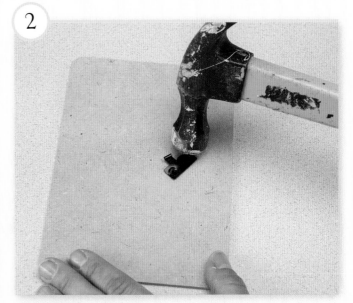

2

Hammer sharp edges
Using the hammer, gently hammer down the edges of any remaining metal.

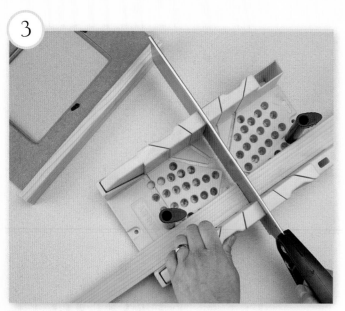

Prepare back wood pieces

Using the pencil and ruler, measure and mark the wood trim to fit on the two side lengths of the back of the frame. Using the saw and the miter box (the miter box is optional), cut the wood trim pieces.

Measure, mark and cut two more pieces that fit within the two side pieces for the top and bottom of the frame.

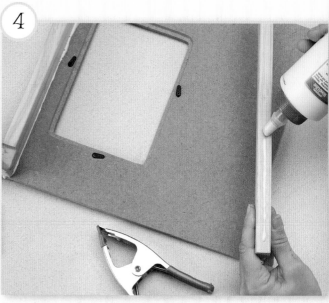

Attach wood pieces to back

Using the sandpaper, smooth the ends of the trim. Apply a generous amount of wood glue to the edge of the trim piece. Using one clamp on each end, secure the trim piece to the frame. It's OK if the glue oozes from the sides, just use a paper towel to wipe away any drips from the outside.

Let the glue dry thoroughly. Repeat this step until all the trim is secured and dry.

Prepare paper clay faces

Using the art doll face molds, push the paper clay into the cavity until the cavity is filled. Gently remove the paper clay face. Repeat for two more faces. Allow the paper clay faces to dry, about 24 hours.

Paint faces

Using the paintbrush, paint the front and sides of each paper clay face with the metallic acrylic paint. (Don't dilute the paint with water when painting the faces—it will make a mess of the clay.) Allow the paint to dry thoroughly.

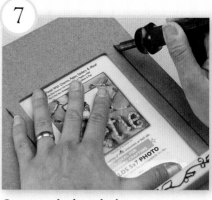

Create window ledge

Following Step 3, measure, mark and cut the trim piece that will serve as the window ledge. Using a medium amount of the glue, adhere the wood piece under the window. Using the paper towel, wipe away any excess glue. Let the wood glue dry thoroughly.

Using the pencil, mark the desired design for the window ledge. Using the wood burning tool, burn the design. When the frame has dried, mark lines on either side of the window ½" (1cm) from the window and burn the lines.

Tip
It doesn't matter if the backs of the faces are perfectly smooth. You can always sand the back once it's dry if you want a smooth finish.

8

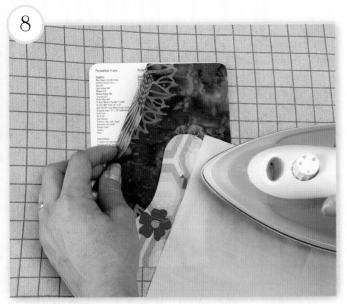

Create design

Measure the dimensions of the frame and incorporate the window as part of the design. Prepare the fabric design elements using the Telamadera Fusion process on pages 17–18.

Open the back of the frame and remove the glass and the cardboard insert from the window. Using the cardboard as a canvas, build the fabric layers for the window. Place the scrap cloth over the window design. Using the iron on the cotton setting, adhere the fabric to the cardboard.

9

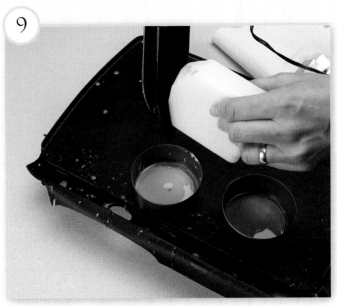

Prepare encaustic medium

Place the fabric-covered cardboard and frame door back in the frame.

Turn the hot plate on to 200°F (93°C). Do not heat the clear encaustic medium above 200°F (93°C). Place the tuna cans on the hot plate. Holding the bar of clear encaustic medium and tacking iron above one of the tuna cans, drip a few drops of green encaustic paint into the can. Add clear encaustic medium to the dilute paint to a transparent consistency. Using the craft stick, stir the encaustic. Repeat this step for the turquoise paint stick using the other tuna can.

10

Add encaustic medium to background

Using the paper towel, wipe any colored encaustic from the iron.

Decide which part of the scrapbook paper you want to use in the background of the art piece. Using the scissors, cut out those pieces.

Holding the bar of clear encaustic and tacking iron above the frame surface, drip a generous amount of wax directly onto the frame, covering the entire area. Then drip wax onto the fabric pieces in the window.

11

Add white encaustic medium

Using the tacking iron, drip the white encaustic medium onto the frame. Avoid dripping the white encaustic on the fabric in the window. Using the tacking iron, gently spread the encaustic to cover as much of the surface as possible. Use the tacking iron to fuse the wax to the surface by lightly dragging it along the surface.

Add paper

Using the paper towel, wipe the white encaustic medium off the tacking iron. Allow the wax to solidify (but not harden). Place the scrapbook paper pieces on top of the wax. Drip another generous amount of the clear wax all over the paper. Using the tacking iron, fuse the wax and paper together.

Scrape wax

Using the tacking iron and clear encaustic, drip more wax within the window. Using a piece of plastic (like an old credit card), gently scrape away the warm wax from the design parts of the paper and the fabric in the window. You are both layering wax and scraping parts of it away to reveal the design. Keep the iron in hand to heat the wax if it gets too hard.

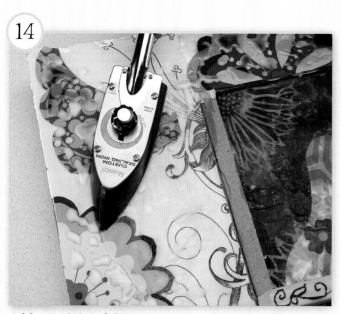

Add remaining fabrics

Arrange the remaining fabrics on top of the scrapbook paper. Using the tacking iron and clear encaustic, drip wax on them. Using the piece of plastic, gently scrape the wax to reveal the fabric designs. (Be sure to scrape gently because it is easy to scrape the fabrics off.) Gently press the iron to the surface to fuse the fabrics in place.

Important: To avoid staining the fabrics with the encaustic paint in the following steps, make sure you have covered all of the fabrics with clear encaustic medium.

Add colored encaustics

Using the tacking iron, drip white encaustic on the window edges and spread.

Using the paper towel, wipe off any white encaustic from the tacking iron. Wearing the oven mitt, drip the green paint from the cans onto the surface where you would like more color.

16

Spread colored encaustic

Using the tacking iron, spread the colored encaustic to the desired places on the art piece. Don't push the iron into the surface; instead gently move the paint around until the desired color materializes. Use the piece of plastic to scrape where needed.

17

Add turquoise encaustic

Clean the surface of the iron with a paper towel. Following Steps 15 and 16, add the blue encaustic.

18

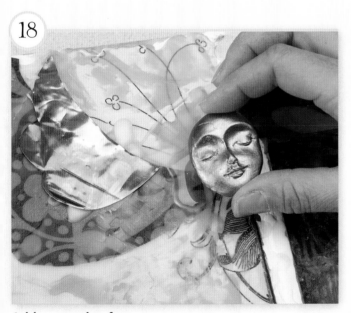

Add paper clay faces

Clean the surface of the iron with a paper towel. If you are incorporating a copper piece into the design: Using the marker, draw the desired design on the copper sheet. Using the metal shears, cut out the copper shape.

Drip a generous amount of the clear encaustic medium to use as glue for the art doll faces and the copper piece. Allow the puddle of wax to cool slightly (it will become faintly cloudy), then push the clay face into the wax. Do not drip wax onto the front of the faces.

You can add wax to the copper but be aware that the copper may lose some shine. Use the plastic card to scrape off excess wax.

19

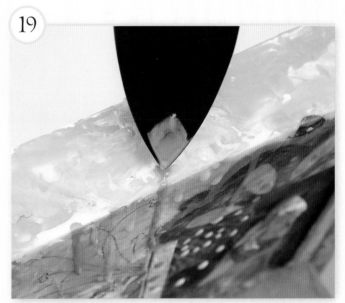

Finish artwork

Using the tacking iron, drip the green encaustic on the window ledge, top, bottom and sides. Heat and scrape the piece until the wood burned design is revealed. Embellish the art with drips of white, green and turquoise paint, adding glitter while the paint is still hot. Do not use the iron on the glitter. Use the same dripping and scraping to complete the sides.

Balance
Beads and Canvas

Mix it up with paints, fabrics and beads on canvas. Beads will entice your viewer to step closer and see what's sparkling. Begin with a loose application of background paint, letting the white of the canvas peek through for light. If you don't feel comfortable painting the figure, outline her silhouette and create her with fabric.

Materials

18" × 24" (46cm × 61cm) canvas
assorted acrylic paints
water
paintbrush
paper
pencil
fine-tipped permanent marker
carbon paper

fabrics
Steam-A-Seam 2 (SAS2)
heavy book that is at least as big as the iron and as tall as the canvas
scrap cloth
iron
sharp embroidery needle with large eye
embroidery floss

beads
dimensional paint
ruler
Phillips-head screwdriver
2 D-rings with mounting brackets
screws that fit the D-rings
6.2mm picture hanging wire
wire cutters

BALANCE

I have a love/spite relationship with yoga. In spite of the strength, balance and peace it brings to my life, it kicks my abs! They say if you can visualize it, it becomes reality. Maybe by painting Balance, *more of it will come into my life!*

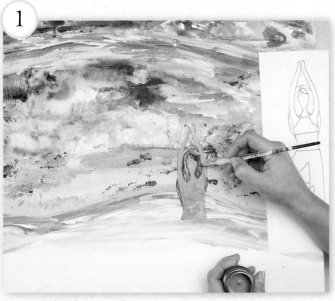

1

Prepare background
Using the paintbrush, loosely paint the canvas background with acrylics and water, using a lighter application in some areas and using thick application of paint for other areas. I kept the bottom of my canvas free of paint as I used a large piece of fabric instead of paint there. Let the paint dry completely.

Using the paper and pencil, draw a figure. When you are pleased with the design, use the marker to trace over it. Using the carbon paper and pencil, transfer your figure drawing to the canvas. Using the paintbrush, paint the parts of the figure you want to paint with acrylics.

2

Prepare fabrics
Prepare the fabric pieces using the Telamadera Fusion process (page 17–18).

3

Prepare for ironing
Place the book under the canvas so the iron has something to press against while you fuse the fabrics to the surface.

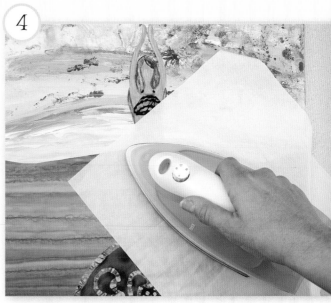

4

Fuse some fabric pieces
Arrange the lower background fabrics and the figure's top on the canvas. Place the piece of scrap cloth over the fabrics. Using the iron on a cotton setting, fuse the fabric to the canvas. Move the book under the canvas as needed.

5

Trace flower stems and vines
Position the figure's pants and the fabric flower pieces. Using the pencil, mark where you want the stems and vines for the flowers.

Tip

For the flowers, I used fabric with repeating floral designs. I placed the slightly larger SAS2 on the shapes I wanted, fused it and then trimmed the shapes to my liking.

6

Paint flower stems and vines

Using the paintbrush, paint the stems and vines in the desired acrylic paint colors. Move the flowers and other elements as needed. Let the paint dry thoroughly.

7

Fuse remaining fabric and add beads

Replace the fabric elements. Place the scrap cloth over the fabric. Using the iron, fuse the fabric to the canvas. Move the book as necessary.

Using the embroidery needle and floss, sew the beads onto the canvas. Use knots on the back of the canvas to secure the beads.

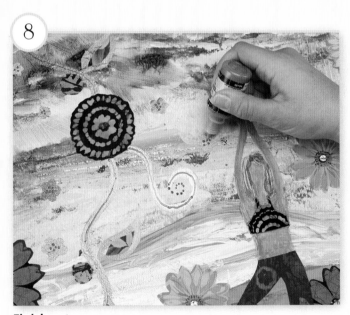

8

Finish art

Apply additional SAS2 flowers and leaves to fill in the design. Using the dimensional paint, embellish the artwork. You can also stitch the canvas with the embroidery floss.

To finish, paint the sides of the canvas black. Add the hardware to the wood sides on the back of the canvas (see Steps 16–17 on page 20).

Sisterhood
Freezer Paper With Paints

The beauty of silkscreen paints is that their transparency allows you to layer them over acrylics, stamps and drawings, and they work well on fabrics, papers, canvas and wood. They are thick, require no water and are wonderful with Telamadera Fusion. This technique is a simpler version of silkscreening, but you can use a silkscreen if desired.

Materials

background fabric, 20" × 22" (51cm × 56cm)	silkscreen paints	painted pieces of paper
stencil (scrapbooking supply)	craft knife	embroidery floss
stencil brush	cutting mat	glue stick
acrylic metallic paint	iron	scrap cloth
pencil	silkscreen (optional)	fabrics
paper	paper plate	Steam-A-Seam 2 (SAS2)
black fine-tipped permanent marker	palette knife or craft stick	¼ yard (¼m) fabric for border
scissors	old credit card	dimensional paint
freezer paper	paper towels	beads or embellishment

SISTERHOOD

"We don't see things as they are, we see them as we are."

—Anaïs Nin

Women are part of a sisterhood. When one rises, we all do. Seeing our own beauty and speaking our truth helps others see theirs. Let's connect like Tibetan prayer flags, waving our intentions for the highest good of all.

1

Stencil background
Using the stencil and stencil brush, apply the stencil design to the background fabric using the acrylic metallic paint. Let the paint dry.

2

Prepare design
Using the pencil, draw your design onto the paper exactly as you would like to see it silkscreened. When you are satisfied with the design, use the black marker to trace over it.

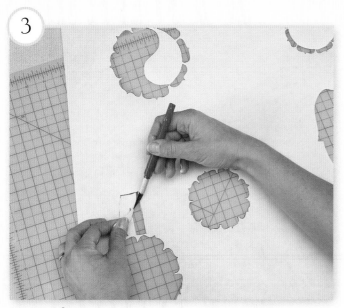

Prepare freezer paper

Using the scissors, cut a piece of freezer paper to the same size as the background fabric. Place the freezer paper on top of the design. Using the black pen, trace the pieces you will use onto the freezer paper with the silkscreen paint, exactly as they will be on the final artwork. You might have to create another freezer paper screen for any parts that overlap.

Using the craft knife, cut out the pieces of freezer paper where you want the silkscreen paints to be applied.

Paint silkscreen design

Using the iron on a cotton setting, iron the freezer paper onto the background fabric, being careful not to tear the freezer paper as you move the iron over the surface. Make sure the paper is completely fused to the fabric. If you are using a silkscreen, lay it over the freezer paper. (For this particular painting method, a traditional silkscreen is optional. Remove it when you are finished painting and wash it immediately.)

Lay out the silkscreen paints on the paper plate. Using the palette knife, apply small amounts of two to three paints to the edge of the credit card. Using the credit card, simultaneously push the paint and spread it over the freezer paper.

Using the paper towels, clean the credit card and palette knife thoroughly. Apply other color combinations onto other areas of the artwork, cleaning the card and palette knife between each pass.

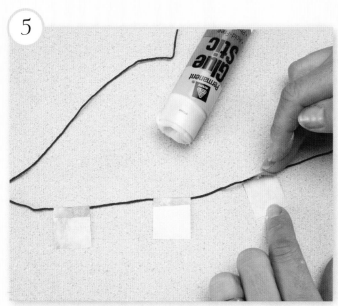

Make prayer flags

Using the scissors, cut the painted pieces of paper to 1" × 1¼" (3cm × 32mm). Using the black pen, write a few words that inspire you. Using the scissors, trim four pieces of the embroidery floss: two long pieces to connect the woman in the middle to the other two women, and two short pieces for the outer women to hold.

Using the glue stick, adhere the painted paper to the embroidery floss by folding the very top edge of the paper over the floss.

Prepare other design elements

Carefully remove the freezer paper to reveal the design. Let the paint dry thoroughly. Place the scrap cloth over the painted surface. Using the iron on a cotton setting, iron over the scrap cloth; the heat will set the paint.

Prepare the fabric pieces using the Telamadera Fusion process (pages 17–18). Arrange the fabric pieces on the artwork.

Coat the underside of the flags and the ends of the embroidery floss with the glue stick. Place the ends of the embroidery floss under the fabric hands and press the flags down to secure them. Using the scissors, trim the embroidery floss as needed. Leave a 5"–6" (13cm–15cm) tail at the ends of the flag lines held by the figures on the sides.

Place the scrap cloth over the hands. Using the iron on the cotton setting, fuse the hands to the background.

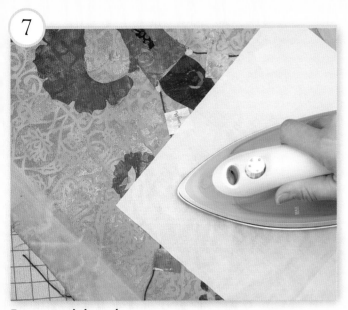

7

Fuse remaining pieces

Place the scrap cloth over the embroidery floss and the remaining fabric pieces. Using the iron on a cotton setting, fuse the floss and fabric to the background. Use a wool setting for any metallic fabrics.

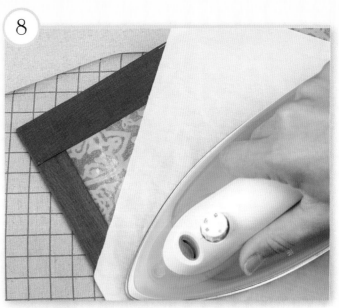

8

Add border

Using the scissors, cut the border fabric into four separate strips of equal width. Prepare the fabric pieces using the Telamadera Fusion process (pages 17–18). Fuse the border fabric to the background fabric of the artwork. For a neater look, fold the edges of the fabric border under. Use the scissors to trim the border fabric as needed. (You can also sew the fabric, without the SAS2, onto the background fabric by hand or with a sewing machine.)

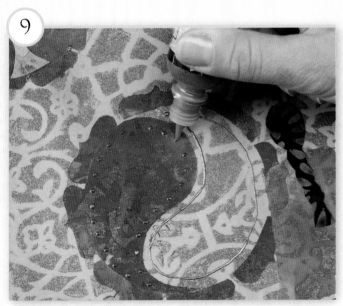

9

Embellish artwork

Let the artwork cool completely. Using the dimensional paint, embellish the artwork. Let the dimensional paint dry completely.

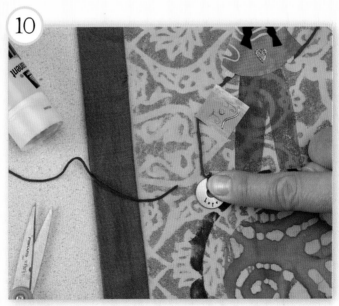

10

Add bead

Tie a knot securing the bead or charm to the end of the prayer flags (held by the women on the outsides). Using the scissors, trim any excess embroidery floss. Using the glue, adhere the bead to the background.

To finish, frame as desired.

Home
Cardstock

This project is an exercise in mixing media that hopefully will inspire you to bring different materials together. There is no end to what can be combined! What techniques can you blend to create something new?

Materials

- paintbrush
- white paint for stamps
- leaf-shaped foam stamps
- colored cardstock or plain colored scrapbook paper
- old credit card
- transparent acrylic paints
- stencil

- stencil brush
- pearlescent white acrylic paint
- fabric
- sewing machine
- paper
- pencil
- threads
- Steam-A-Seam 2 (SAS2)

- 14" × 14" (36cm × 36cm) piece of light-weight interfacing
- scrap cloth
- iron
- dimensional paint
- 12" × 12" (30cm × 30cm) plain craft frame
- wood burning tool
- scissors

HOME

"Where thou art—that—is Home."
—Emily Dickinson

If home is inside each of us, then my imagination has a huge, bright, color-ful studio inside that home with great big windows and an endless supply of materials that I can play with. Oh, and a lap pool! If your imagination had a room in your inner home, what would it be like? What's brewing in there?

Decorate cardstock
Using the paintbrush, apply the white paint to the leaf-shaped foam stamps. Stamp the cardstock as desired. Let the stamped images dry. Using the credit card, apply a small amount of the transparent acrylic paint or silkscreen paint by scraping the paint onto the cardstock. Let the paint dry.

Prepare fabric for tree
Using the paper and pencil, prepare a free-hand tree design. Using the stencil, stencil brush and pearlescent white paint, decorate the fabric. Let the paint dry completely.

Sew leaf design

Using the sewing machine on a regular stitch setting, free-motion stitch a leaf design onto the purple fabric.

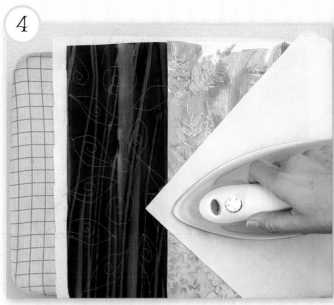

Fuse background fabrics

Prepare all the fabric pieces and the cardstock using the Telamadera Fusion process (see pages 17–18, steps 8–11) backing pieces with SAS2. Arrange the background fabrics on the interfacing so they overlap the cardstock. Place the scrap cloth over the background. Using the iron on a cotton setting, fuse the background fabrics to the interfacing.

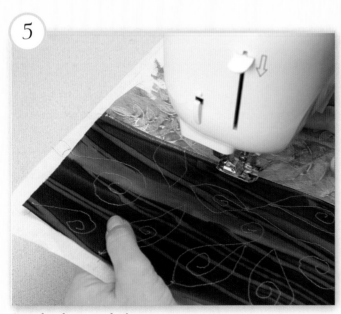

Sew background pieces

Using the sewing machine set to satin stitch, sew the cardstock and fabric pieces along the vertical length of the artwork.

Tip

If you're using metallic threads, use interfacing under the fabric when you sew it. Also, practice! Metallic threads have their own personalities, so practicing on scrap fabric (with the interfacing) will go a long way.

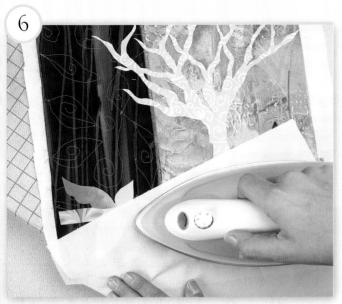

6

Add remaining fabric elements

Arrange the remaining fabric pieces on the background. Place the scrap cloth over these pieces. Using the iron on a cotton setting (wool setting for metallic fabrics), fuse the fabrics to the background.

7

Embellish artwork

Using the sewing machine, add stitches to the artwork. You can also use dimensional paint.

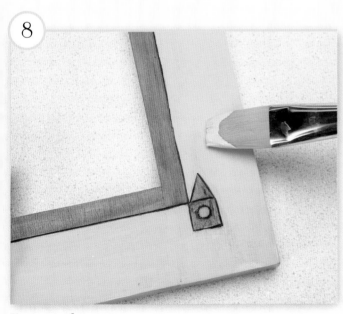

8

Decorate frame

Using the wood burning tool, the paintbrush and paints, decorate the frame to complement the artwork. After framing the artwork, use the scissors to trim away any excess interfacing.

Detail

The Key is Passion
Architectural Wood Elements

Architectural wood elements are lightweight, inexpensive and detailed. They create relief in your artwork and can help emphasize a theme. This project uses papers cut from magazines and scrapbook papers with a piece of lace for the woman's skirt.

Materials

12" x 12" (30cm × 30cm) wood panel	scissors	scrap cloth
fine grit sandpaper	rubber stamp	iron
paper	permanent metallic ink pad	dimensional paint
pencil	architectural wood elements (available at craft stores or building supply store)	plastic half crystals, 3 clear and 2 small pink
scrapbook paper	magazines	hot glue gun
paintbrush	fabrics, including lace	button
acrylic paints, including metallic paints	Steam-A-Seam 2 (SAS2)	reproduction antique key
ruler		Aleene's 7800 adhesive

THE KEY IS PASSION

If enthusiasm brings joy to what we do, then passion kicks it up to bliss. We hold the key to our happiness and only we can unlock the door to our creativity. I like to imagine myself on a creative threshold before beginning a project. I wonder what new insight lies beyond the door. Let's let passion be our guide.

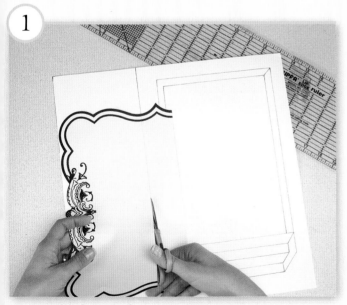

1

Prepare background
Using the sandpaper, smooth the wood panel. Design the artwork, incorporating scrapbook paper into the design. Using the paintbrush and acrylic paints, paint the entire background. Let the paint dry thoroughly. Using the ruler and pencil, measure and mark the paper according to the design specifications. Using the scissors, cut the paper to size.

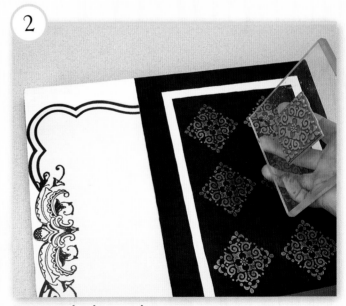

2

Decorate background
Prepare the paper piece using the Telamadera Fusion process (page 17–18), backing them with the SAS2. Using the rubber stamp, decorate the background on the door with the metallic stamp ink. Let the ink dry.

Paint wood pieces

Using the paintbrush, paint the architectural wood elements with the black, metallic and white paints. Let the paint dry thoroughly.

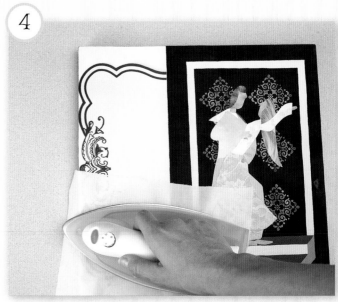

Add magazine pieces

Go through the magazines to find papers to serve as skin, hair and clothing for the figures. Cut pieces larger than you'll need. Prepare the designed paper and fabric pieces using the Telamadera Fusion process (pages 17–18). Arrange them on the artwork surface. Place the scrap cloth over the paper pieces. Using the iron on a wool setting, fuse the pieces to the background.

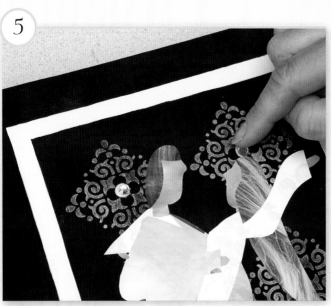

Add crystals

Using the dimensional paint, adhere the clear half crystals to the center of the stamped design on the door by gently pushing them into the paint.

Add door knob

Repeat Step 5 to add the pink crystals to the woman's shoes. Using the hot glue gun, adhere the button door knob to the background.

Tip

You can bring together all sorts of craft supplies to create a unique look. For the woman's skirt, I use pink scrapbook paper and lace, both backed with the SAS2. Sift through your art stashes and see what colors and textures strike your fancy—bringing elements together on your work surface can inspire something wonderful.

Embellish artwork

Using the hot glue gun, adhere the key to the background. Using Aleene's 7800 adhesive, glue the architectural wood elements to the background. Let the adhesives dry thoroughly. Using the dimensional paint, embellish the artwork as desired.

Detail

Sacred Spaces
Heavy Gel With Cardstock

When I think of this project, I think of dessert! Spreading the heavy gel for this artwork is just like spreading icing on a cake. Just don't lick the palette knife!

Materials

paper
pencil
black fine-tipped permanent marker
paintbrush
white acrylic paint
art board
rub-on transfers with stylus
latex gloss
palette knife

extra heavy gel (matte)
lace cardstock (scrapbook supply)
fabrics
Steam-A-Seam 2 (SAS2)
Teflon pressing sheet
iron
contact paper
scissors
palette

transparent acrylics
craft knife
paper towels
dimensional paint
Phillips-head screwdriver
2 D-rings with mounting brackets
screws that fit the D-rings
6.2mm picture hanging wire
wire cutters

SACRED SPACES

"Your sacred space is where you can find yourself again and again."

—Joseph Campbell

People-made things began first as thoughts. The computer I sit at (crazy, brilliant invention), the coffeemaker working on its next pot (thank you!) and all the amazing artwork in the world came from an inspired place within each inventor. We are our own living, breathing sacred space with potential and promise to create whatever we can dream up. How fun is that?

Sketch design
Using the pencil, sketch the overall design of the layout and specific design shapes you will use on the paper. When you are satisfied with the design, use the black marker to trace over it.

Prepare background
Using the paintbrush, apply the white paint to the art board. Let the paint dry. Using the pencil, lightly sketch the design lines onto the art board. (This helps you see how the surface is divided.) Following the package directions, add the rub-on transfers to the background.

3

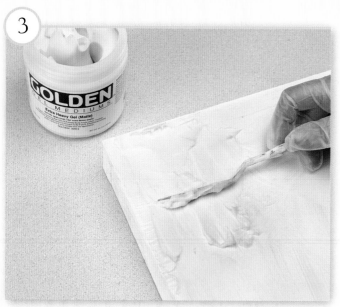

Add gel

Put on the gloves. Using the palette knife, apply a generous coating of the gel to the surface only in the section where the lace cardstock will go.

4

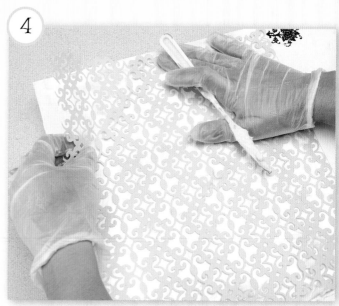

Add lace cardstock

Lay the lace cardstock onto the gel. Using your hands, gently press the cardstock into the gel.

5

Add more gel

Using the palette knife, add more gel to the surface of the lace cardstock to secure it. Let the gel dry completely.

6

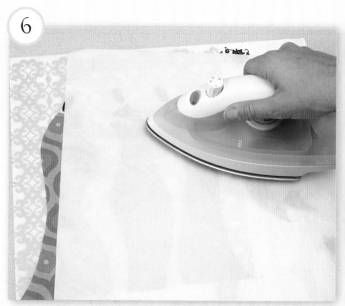

Add fabric pieces

Prepare the fabric pieces using the Telamadera Fusion process (page 18), backing the fabric with SAS2. Arrange them on the surface. Place a Teflon sheet over the fabric pieces. Using the iron on a wool setting, fuse the fabrics to the background.

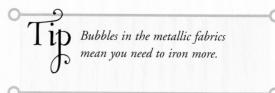

Tip *Bubbles in the metallic fabrics mean you need to iron more.*

7

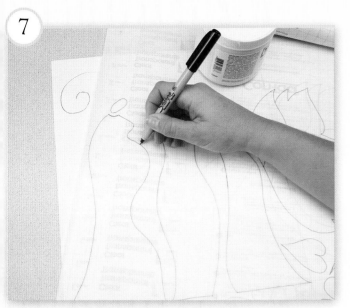

Prepare contact paper

Using the black pen, trace the designs from the original drawing onto the contact paper.

8

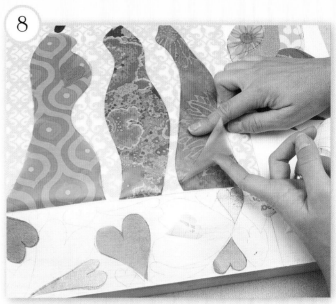

Apply contact paper

Using the scissors, cut out the contact paper pieces. One at a time, remove the paper backing from the contact paper pieces and place them, tacky-side down, onto the corresponding fabric pieces. Using your finger, smooth the contact paper.

9

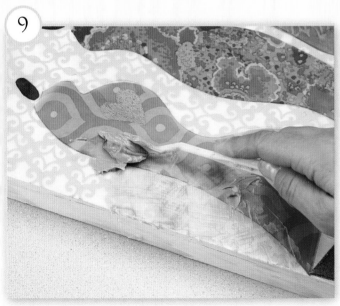

Apply paints

On the palette, mix the gel and transparent paints. Using the palette knife, spread the gel colors over the background. Don't push the palette knife against the edges of the fabric, but rather paint slightly over the edge of the contact paper, moving outward.

Tip

If you're unsure where the design from Step 1 should go, use carbon paper to transfer the design onto the surface.

Mix colors
If desired, use the palette knife to blend the paint colors.

Remove contact paper
While the gel is still wet, use the craft knife to carefully lift a corner of the contact paper. Peel the contact paper off of the fabric pieces and discard the contact paper. Using the paper towels, clean the craft knife and the sides of the art board.

Continue painting
Continue applying the gel paints to the other sections of the piece. When you are finished painting, remove the contact paper. Let the surface dry completely.

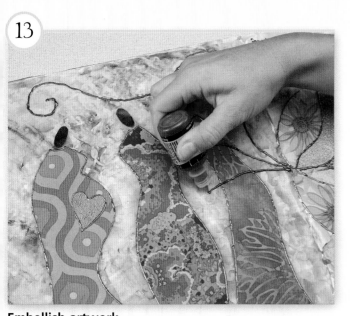

13

Embellish artwork
Using the dimensional paint, embellish the surface. Let the dimensional paint dry completely.

14

Finish artwork
To finish, paint the edges of the artwork black. Add hardware to the wood sides on the back of the canvas (see Steps 16–17 on page 20).

Detail

Coming Home
Bring Wood to Quilt

Why wood on a quilt? Well, why not? Different textures make artwork interesting, and quilts are no exception. Wood craft shapes have a flat, hard surface that make them ideal for stamping detailed rubber stamp images like this one. The finished size of the main body of this quilt is 14" (36cm) square.

Materials

scissors

16" × 16" (41cm × 41cm) piece of fabric for quilt front

14" × 14" (36cm × 36cm) piece of fabric for quilt back

Steam-A-Seam 2 (SAS2)

fabrics for elements

fabric for bottom piece hanging off quilt

iron

sewing machine

threads

16" × 16" (41cm × 41cm) lightweight interfacing

straight pins

scrapbook paper

stamps

stamping ink

colored pens

paintbrush

acrylic paint

4" (10cm) wood craft square

glue stick

three ½" (1cm) craft wood squares

scrap cloth

two 1" (3cm) craft wood squares

three 2" (5cm) craft wood squares

drill with ¹⁄₁₆" (2mm) bit

dimensional paint

embroidery needle

embroidery floss

beads

tiny stick

large tree branch

COMING HOME

Not only can you hang beads (or jewelry findings) from them, but the craft pieces also make interesting focal points for a Nine-Patch wall hanging, or any square-shaped quilt block. Create interest with nine circle-shaped blocks and place a wood craft piece inside each circle. Remember they can be used for jewelry, too (see page 74). How about a small quilt block design to hang as a pendant?

Tip

If you want to make a different sized quilt, cut the fabric for the top sleeve at least 4" (10cm) smaller than the main quilt body. When it is folded in Step 3, 2"–3" (5cm–8cm) should come out of the top of the quilt.

1

Prepare main fabrics
Using the scissors, cut the front fabric, back fabric and the SAS2 to 14" × 14" (36cm × 36cm).

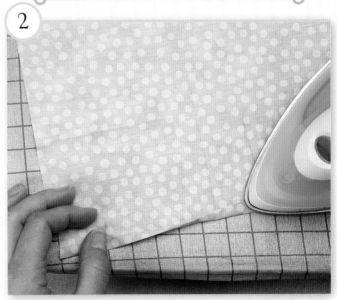

2

Prepare hanging sleeve
Using the scissors, cut the piece of fabric for the sleeve into a 10" × 10" (25cm × 25cm) square. Using the iron, press a ¼" (6mm) seam on two opposing sides of the fabric. Fold the ironed edges over and press again.

3

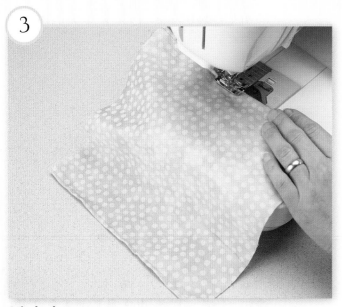

Stitch sleeve seam

Using the sewing machine, stitch along the ironed edges to secure them.

4

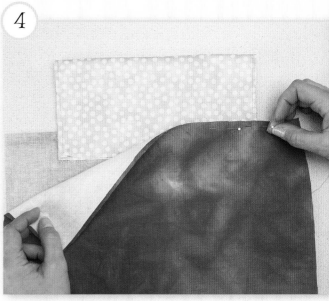

Create quilt sandwich

Repeat Steps 2–3 to create the smaller fabric piece that hangs from the bottom of the quilt.

Place the backing fabric right side down. Remove both paper sides from the SAS2 and place it over the background fabric. Place the top fabric, right side up, on the SAS2.

Fold the sleeve in half, right-side-out, with the raw edges meeting. Place the sleeve between the back fabric and the interfacing, with at least 1" (3cm) of the raw edge from the top of the quilt. Using the straight pins, secure all the layers of the quilt sandwich.

5

Fuse and embellish fabrics

Repeat the final part of Step 4 to secure the smaller piece of fabric that hangs from the bottom.

Prepare the fabric pieces of the design following the Telamadera Fusion process (pages 17–18), backing them with the SAS2. Add these fabric pieces to the top of the quilt sandwich. Using the iron, fuse all the layers together.

Using the sewing machine, satin stitch around the edges of those fabric elements you want to highlight. Change the thread colors as needed.

6

Embellish scrap paper

Using the scissors, trim the piece of scrapbook paper to a 3¾" (10cm) square. Using the stamps and stamping ink, layer the design onto the paper. Using the colored pens, embellish the stamp figure.

7

Decorate large craft wood

Using the paintbrush, paint the 4" (10cm) craft wood piece. Allow it to dry thoroughly. Using the glue stick, secure the embellished scrapbook paper to the craft wood.

Paint and embellish the three ½" (1cm) craft wood squares as desired. If fusing fabric to the wood pieces, use a scrap cloth between the wood and the iron. Fuse any desired fabrics to the larger wood piece. Using the glue stick, adhere the smaller squares to the larger one.

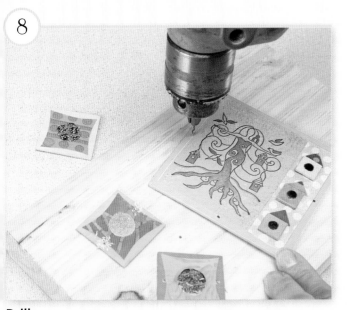

8

Drill

Repeat Step 8 to decorate the 1" (3cm) and 2" (5cm) craft wood pieces.

Using the drill with the 1/16" (2mm) bit, drill holes on opposing sides of the large piece of craft wood and the three 2" (5cm) pieces.

9

Secure wood pieces

Using the sewing machine set to a satin stitch, sew around the entire edge of the quilt. Remove the straight pins as needed.

Using the dimensional paint, embellish the quilt and wood squares as desired. Allow the paint to dry thoroughly.

Using the embroidery needle and floss, secure the wood pieces to the quilt. Tie knots on the back of the quilt to secure the wood pieces.

10

Embellish quilt

Using the embroidery needle and threads, add any desired beads to the artwork. Knot the floss on the back of the quilt to secure it.

11

Continue embellishing

Using the embroidery needle and thread, continue embellishing the quilt with beads and the small stick.

12

Finish quilt

Run the large branch through the top sleeve of the quilt. This branch will let you hang the quilt.

> *Tip*
>
> *Branches are beautiful objects to pair with fabric quilt hangings and are so easy to find—just go for a walk in the park! When looking for the perfect branch, find one that is strong. You'll want a branch that is a few inches longer on both sides of the sleeve, so if you find a branch you think is too long, you can always cut it down to size. If needed, strip the branch of any loose pieces of bark. You can also use sandpaper to smooth the branch's surface if you'd like a more polished look.*

Flowers
Heavy Gel Outline

By adding thickeners like heavy gel to acrylic paints, we can create an oil paint-like effect. You can pre-mix acrylic paints with heavy gel or build up a layer of heavy gel first, as shown, before adding the paint layers. Have fun inventing flowers!

Materials

paper	12" × 12" (30cm × 30cm) scrapbook paper
pencil	Steam-A-Seam 2 (SAS2)
black fine-tipped permanent marker	scrap cloth
acrylic paints	iron
medium paintbrush	palette knife
art board	heavy gel (matte)
rub-on transfers with stylus	dimensional paint
fabrics	

FLOWERS

"The earth laughs in flowers."

—Ralph Waldo Emerson

This piece is my take on impasto (from the Italian word paste*), an art technique where paint is thickly laid on the art surface. My favorite abstract expressionist painter, Joan Mitchell (1925–1992), created a dance of color in the thick and multilayered canvases she created with oil paints.*

Complete design
Using the black marker and paper, design the artwork, dividing the composition into different planes. Draw all of the fabric elements.

Prepare background
Using the paintbrush, paint the art board with the acrylic paints, following the design from Step 1 to divide the surface. Let the paint dry. Following the package directions, add the rub-on transfers. Save some to fill in any spaces later.

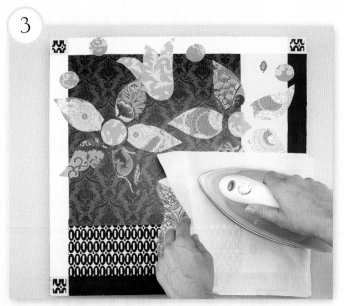

Add fabric pieces

Prepare the fabric and paper pieces using the Telamadera Fusion process (pages 17–18), backing them with SAS2.

Arrange the fabric shapes on the background. Place the scrap cloth over the fabric pieces. Using the iron on a cotton setting, fuse the fabric to the background.

Add heavy gel outline

Using the palette knife, create a rough outline around the fabric pieces with a generous amount of heavy gel. Let the heavy gel dry completely. The dry gel will be slightly cloudy.

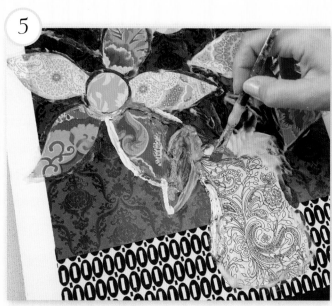

Paint heavy gel outline

Using the paintbrush, paint acrylics on top of the heavy gel. If needed, mix the paints with more heavy gel to thicken the outline. Layer the paint colors for dimension and texture.

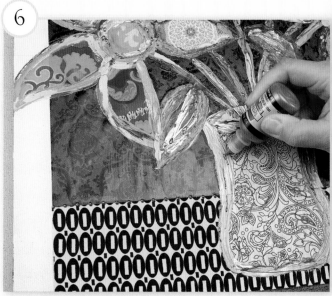

Embellish artwork

Let the paint dry thoroughly. If desired, add more rub-ons. Using the dimensional paint, embellish the artwork.

Tip

Don't be afraid to mix and match textures and supplies. The background of this piece was created with paint, scrapbook paper and fabric. I love how the flowers seem to pop off of the art board. The graphic fabric and the subtle paper make a beautiful backdrop for these lovely blooms.

Gallery

IN THE DOORWAY OF POSSIBILITY
Encaustic with fabric, metal, paper clay and wood craft pieces

SAN FRANCISCO GIRL WITH FLOWERS IN HER HAIR
Heavy acrylics with fabric, 3-D paint

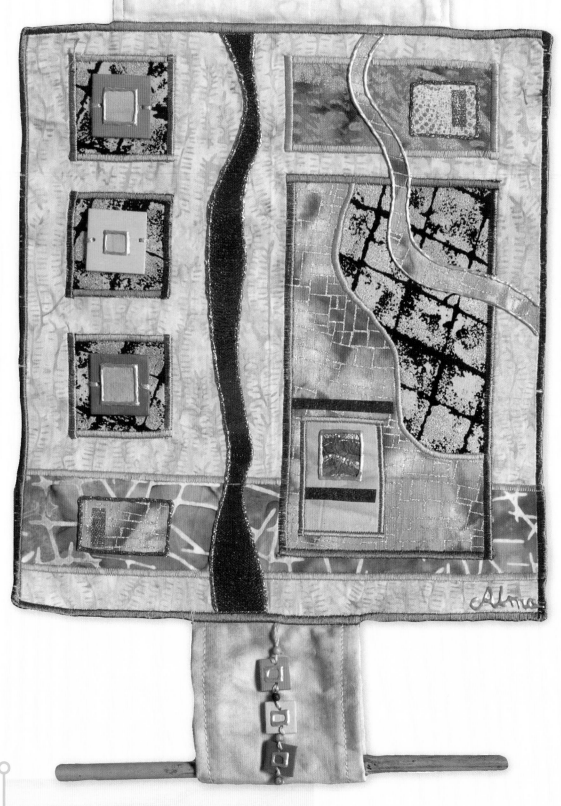

IN KEEPING WITH YESTERDAY
Small quilt with wood craft pieces and 3-D paint

CASITA
Small quilt with wood craft pieces, metal and 3-D paint

WALKING TOWARD MY WISDOM
Crackle paint, fabric, paper lace and heavy gel

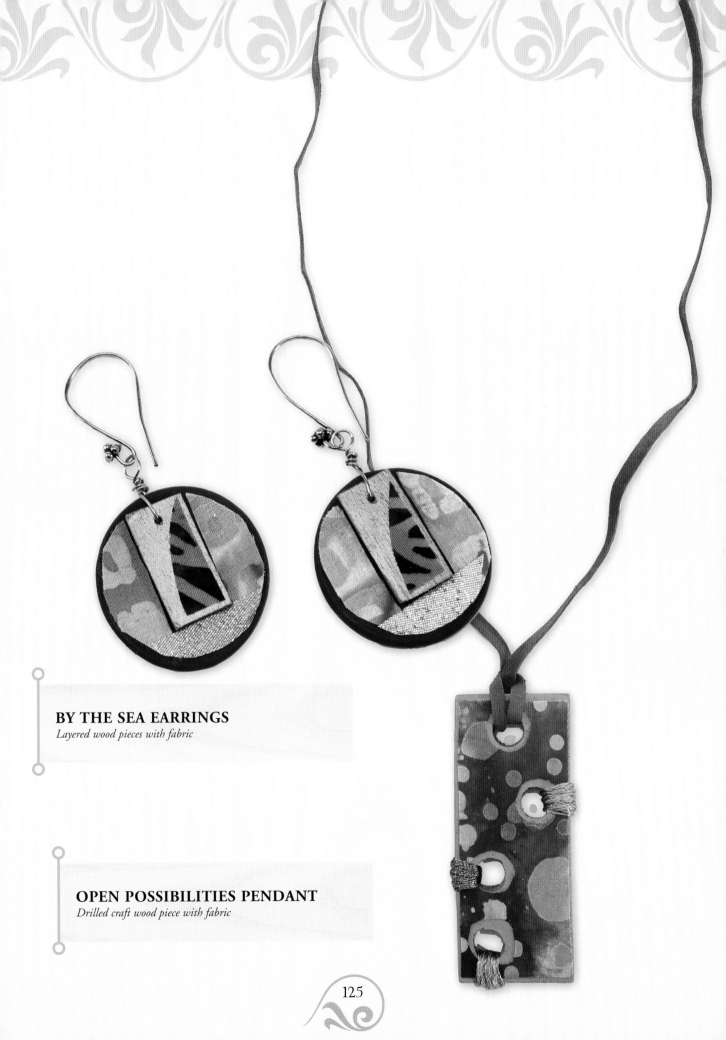

BY THE SEA EARRINGS
Layered wood pieces with fabric

OPEN POSSIBILITIES PENDANT
Drilled craft wood piece with fabric

125

Resources

All of the materials used in the techniques and projects in this book can be purchased online or at your local craft, fabric, hardware, home improvement, scrapbooking and rubber-stamping stores.

ALMA ART
www.almaart.com
rubber stamps

CLEARSNAP
www.clearsnap.com
rubber stamp ink pads

WALNUT HOLLOW
www.walnuthollow.com
pre-routed wood plaques, wood burning tool

SKIL
www.skiltools.com
power tools

THE WARM COMPANY
www.warmcompany.com
Steam–A–Seam 2

GOLDEN ARTIST COLORS, INC.
www.goldenpaints.com
acrylic paint, gel mediums

LIQUITEX
www.liquitex.com
High Gloss Varnish, acrylic paint

PURDY
www.purdycorp.com
brushes for varnishing

KI MEMORIES
www.kimemories.com
scrapbook supplies

K&COMPANY
www.kandcompany.com
scrapbook supplies

ANNA GRIFFIN
www.annagriffin.com
paper

PELLON
www.pellonideas.com
interfacing

SULKY
www.sulky.com
threads

DUNCAN ENTERPRISES
www.duncancrafts.com
Aleene's 7800 adhesive, Scribbles 3-D paint

SAKURA COLOR PRODUCTS OF AMERICA
www.gellyroll.com
pens

SHARPIE
www.sharpie.com
permanent pens

CRYSTALLIZED SWAROVSKI ELEMENTS
www.swarovski.com/crystallized
half crystals with flat backs

STAMPENDOUS!
www.stampendous.com
glitter

MARTHA'S GOURDS
www.marthasgourds.com
clean, hollowed gourds

KAREN'S WHIMSY
www.karenswhimsy.com
copyright-free images

FORSTER CRAFT
www.homecrafting.com/forster/craft/products.html
Woodsies and wood craft products

HOUSTON ART, INC.
www.houstonart.com
metal leaf

JUNE TAILOR, INC.
www.junetailor.com
Teflon pressing sheet

EPSON
www.epson.com
matte photo paper

EMBELLISHMENT VILLAGE
www.embellishmentvillage.com
Angelina Fibers

JACQUARD
www.jacquardproducts.com
Lumiere paints (metallic), Versatex Screen Printing Inks

DELTA CREATIVE
www.deltacreative.com
crackle medium, paint

PLAID
www.plaidonline.com
paint

FREDRIX
www.taramaterials.com
archival art canvas

R&F HANDMADE PAINTS
www.rfpaints.com
encaustic medium and encaustic paint

HOBBICO
www.hobbico.com
Sealing Iron (for Encaustic)

CREATIVE PAPERCLAY
www.paperclay.com
Creative Paperclay

DARICE
www.darice.com
frames

AMERICAN CRAFTS
www.americancrafts.com
rub-on transfers

ARTISTIC WOODWORKING, INC.
www.artwood.com
architectural wood pieces

THE ENCHANTED GALLERY
www.theenchantedgallery.com
doll face molds

ADDITIONAL COPYRIGHT-FREE IMAGE SOURCES:
www.antiqueclipart.com
www.bigfoto.com
www.doverpublications.com

Index

Find creative collage inspiration with these titles from North Light Books

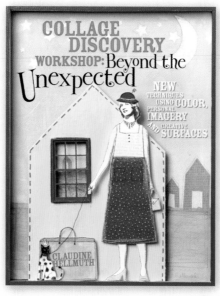

Image Transfer Workshop
By Darlene Olivia McElroy and Sandra Duran Wilson

Learn 35 transfer techniques (complete with finished art examples) that cover everything from basic tape and gel medium transfers to much more advanced techniques. McElroy's and Wilson's troubleshooting fixes will even enable you to work with your transfers that don't quite live up to expectations. *Image Transfer Workshop* provides a quick reference and examples of art using a variety of techniques that will inspire you to go beyond single transfer applications.

ISBN-10: 1-60061-160-5
ISBN-13: 978-1-60061-160-5
paperback, 128 pages, Z2509

Collage Discovery Workshop: Beyond the Unexpected
By Claudine Hellmuth

In a follow-up to her first workshop book, Claudine Hellmuth taps into a whole new level of creativity in *Beyond the Unexpected*. Inside you'll find original artwork and inventive ideas that show you how to personalize your own collage pieces using new techniques and interesting surfaces. In addition, the extensive gallery compiled by Claudine and other top collage artists will spark your imagination. Whether you're a beginner or a collage veteran, you'll enjoy this lovely book both as inspiration and as a practical guide.

ISBN 10: 1-58180-678-7
ISBN 13: 978-1-58180-678-6
paperback, 128 pages, 33267

Collage Unleashed
By Traci Bautista

Learn to collage using everything but the kitchen sink with this bright and playful book. Author Traci Bautista shows you there are no mistakes in making art. You can combine anything—from paper, fabric, paint and even paper towels to beads, metal, doodles and stitching to create unique art books, fabric journals and mixed media paintings. The book includes detailed instructions for lots of innovative techniques, such as staining/dying paper towels, freestyle hand lettering, doodling, funky embroidery and crayon transfers. Then you'll learn how to turn your newfound techniques into dazzling projects.

ISBN-10: 1-58180-845-3
ISBN-13: 978-1-58180-845-2
paperback, 128 pages, Z0024

These and other fine North Light titles are available at your local craft retailer, bookstore or online supplier, or visit our Web site at www.mycraftivitystore.com.